A Treatise of the Fear of God

"BLESSED IS EVERY ONE T
128:1

"FEAR GOD."–REVELATION 14:7

This exhortation is not only found here in the text, but is in several other places of the Scripture pressed, and that with much vehemency, upon the children of men, as in Ecclesiastes 12:13; 1 Peter 1:17, &c. I shall not trouble you with a long preamble, or forespeech to the matter, nor shall I here so much as meddle with the context, but shall immediately fall upon the words themselves, and briefly treat of the fear of God. The text, you see, presenteth us with matter of greatest moment, to wit, with God, and with the fear of him.

First they present us with God, the true and living God, maker of the worlds, and upholder of all things by the word of his power: that incomprehensible majesty, in comparison of whom all nations are less than the drop of a bucket, and than the small dust of the balance. This is he that fills heaven and earth, and is everywhere present with the children of men, beholding the evil and the good; for he hath set his eyes upon all their ways.

So that, considering that by the text we have presented to our souls the Lord God and Maker of us all, who also will be either our Saviour or Judge, we are in reason and duty bound to give the more earnest heed to the things that shall be spoken, and be the more careful to receive them, and put them in practice; for, as I said, as they present us with the mighty God, so they exhort us to the highest duty towards him; to wit, to fear him. I call it the highest duty, because it is, as I may call it, not only a duty in itself, but, as it were, the salt that seasoneth every duty. For there is no duty performed by us that can by any means be accepted of God, if it be not seasoned with godly fear. Wherefore the apostle saith, "Let us have grace, whereby we may serve God acceptably, with reverence and godly fear." Of this fear, I say, I would discourse at this time; but because this word fear is variously taken in the Scripture, and because it may be profitable to us to see it in its variety, I shall therefore choose this method for the managing of my discourse, even to show you the nature of the word in its several, especially of the chiefest, acceptations. FIRST. Then by this word fear we are to understand even God himself, who is the object of our fear. SECOND. By this word fear we are to understand the Word of God, the rule and director of our fear. Now to speak to this word fear, as it is thus taken.

THIS WORD FEAR AS TAKEN FOR GOD HIMSELF.

FIRST. Of this word "fear," AS IT RESPECTETH GOD HIMSELF, who is the object of our fear.

By this word fear, as I said, we are to understand God himself, who is the object of our fear: For the Divine majesty goeth often under this very name himself. This name Jacob called him by, when he and Laban chid together on Mount Gilead, after that Jacob had made his escape to his father's house; "Except," said he, "the God of my father, the God of Abraham, and the fear of Isaac had been with me, surely thou hadst sent me away now empty." So again, a little after, when Jacob and Laban agree to make a covenant of peace each with other, though Laban, after the jumbling way of the heathen by his oath, puts the true God and the false together, yet "Jacob sware by the fear of his father Isaac" (Gen 31:42,53).

By the fear, that is, by the God of his father Isaac. And, indeed, God may well be called the fear of his people, not only because they have by his grace made him the object of their fear, but because of the dread and terrible majesty that is in him. "He is a mighty God, a great and terrible, and with God is terrible majesty" (Dan 7:28, 10:17; Neh 1:5, 4:14, 9:32; Job 37:22). Who knows the power of his anger? "The mountains quake at him, the hills melt, and the earth is burned at his presence, yea, the world, and all that dwell therein. Who can stand before his indignation? who can abide in the fierceness of his anger? his fury is poured out like fire, and the rocks are thrown down by him" (Nahum 1:5,6). His people know him, and have his dread upon them, by virtue whereof there is begot and maintained in them that godly awe and reverence of his majesty which is agreeable to their profession of him. "Let him be your fear, and let him be your dread." Set his majesty before the eyes of your souls, and let his excellency make you afraid with godly fear (Isa 8:13).

There are these things that make God to be the fear of his people.

First. His presence is dreadful, and that not only his presence in common, but his special, yea, his most comfortable and joyous presence. When God comes to bring a soul news of mercy and salvation, even that visit, that presence of God, is fearful. When Jacob went from Beersheba towards Haran, he met with God in the way by a dream, in the which he apprehended a ladder set upon the earth, whose top reached to heaven; now in this dream, from the top of this ladder, he saw the Lord, and heard him speak unto him, not threateningly; not as having his fury come up into his face; but in the most sweet and gracious manner, saluting him with promise of goodness after promise of goodness, to the number of eight or nine; as will appear if you read the place. Yet I say, when he awoke, all the grace that discovered itself in this heavenly vision to him could not keep him from dread and fear of God's majesty. "And Jacob awaked out of his sleep, and he said, Surely the Lord is in this place, and I knew it not; and he was afraid and said, How dreadful is this place! this is none other but the house of God, and this is the gate of heaven" (Gen 28:10-17).

At another time, to wit, when Jacob had that memorable visit from God, in which he gave him power as a prince to prevail with him; yea, and gave him a name, that by his remembering it he might call God's favour the better to his mind; yet even then and there such dread of the majesty of God was upon him, that he went away wondering that his life was preserved (Gen 32:30). Man crumbles to dust at the presence of God; yea, though he shows himself to us in his robes of salvation. We have read how dreadful and how terrible even the presence of angels have been unto men, and that when they have brought them good tidings from heaven (Judg 13:22; Matt 28:4; Mark 16:5,6). Now, if angels, which are but creatures, are, through the glory that God has put upon them, so fearful and terrible in their appearance to men, how much more dreadful and terrible must God himself be to us, who are but dust and ashes! When Daniel had the vision of his salvation sent him from heaven, for so it was, "O Daniel," said the messenger, "a man greatly beloved" ; yet behold the dread and terror of the person speaking fell with that weight upon this good man's soul, that he could not stand, nor bear up under it. He stood trembling, and cries out, "O my lord, by the vision my sorrows are turned upon me, and I have retained no strength. For how can the servant of this my lord talk with this my lord? for as for me, straightway there remained no strength in me" (Dan 10:16-17). See you here if the presence of God is not a dreadful and a fearful thing; yea, his most gracious and merciful appearances; how much more then when he showeth himself to us as one that disliketh our ways, as one that is offended with us for our sins?

And there are three things that in an eminent manner make his presence dreadful to us.

1. The first is God's own greatness and majesty; the discovery of this, or of himself thus, even as no poor mortals are able to conceive of him, is altogether unsupportable. The man dies to whom he thus discovers himself. "And when I saw him," says John, "I fell at his feet as dead" (Rev 1:17). It was this, therefore, that Job would have avoided in the day that he would have approached unto him. "Let not thy dread," says he, "make me afraid. Then call thou, and I will answer; or let me speak, and answer thou me" (Job

13:21,22). But why doth Job after this manner thus speak to God? Why! it was from a sense that he had of the dreadful majesty of God, even the great and dreadful God that keepeth covenant with his people. The presence of a king is dreadful to the subject, yea, though he carries it never so condescendingly; if then there be so much glory and dread in the presence of the king, what fear and dread must there be, think you, in the presence of the eternal God?

2. When God giveth his presence to his people, that his presence causeth them to appear to themselves more what they are, than at other times, by all other light, they can see. "O my lord," said Daniel, "by the vision my sorrows are turned upon me" ; and why was that, but because by the glory of that vision, he saw his own vileness more than at other times. So again: "I was left alone," says he, "and saw this great vision" ; and what follows? Why, "and there remained no strength in me; for my comeliness was turned into corruption, and I retained no strength" (Dan 10:8,16). By the presence of God, when we have it indeed, even our best things, our comeliness, our sanctity and righteousness, all do immediately turn to corruption and polluted rags. The brightness of his glory dims them as the clear light of the shining sun puts out the glory of the fire or candle, and covers them with the shadow of death. See also the truth of this in that vision of the prophet Isaiah. "Wo is me," said he, "for I am undone, because I am a man of unclean lips, and I dwell in the midst of a people of unclean lips." Why, what is the matter? how came the prophet by this sight? Why, says he, "mine eyes have seen the King, the Lord of hosts" (Isa 6:5). But do you think that this outcry was caused by unbelief? No; nor yet begotten by slavish fear. This was to him the vision of his Saviour, with whom also he had communion before (vv 2-5). It was the glory of that God with whom he had now to do, that turned, as was noted before of Daniel, his comeliness in him into corruption, and that gave him yet greater sense of the disproportion that was betwixt his God and him, and so a greater sight of his defiled and polluted nature.

3. Add to this the revelation of God's goodness, and it must needs make his presence dreadful to us; for when a poor defiled creature shall see that this great God hath, notwithstanding his greatness, goodness in his heart, and mercy to bestow upon him: this makes his presence yet the more dreadful. They "shall fear the Lord and his goodness" (Hosea 3:5). The goodness as well as the greatness of God doth beget in the heart of his elect an awful reverence of his majesty. "Fear ye not me? saith the Lord; will ye not tremble at my presence?" And then, to engage us in our soul to the duty, he adds one of his wonderful mercies to the world, for a motive, "Fear ye not me?" Why, who are thou? He answers, Even I, "which have" set, or "placed the sand for the bound of the sea by a perpetual decree, that it cannot pass it; and though

the waves thereof toss themselves, yet can they not prevail; though they roar, yet can they not pass over it?" (Jer 5:22). Also, when Job had God present with him, making manifest the goodness of his great heart to him, what doth he say? how doth he behave himself in his presence? "I have heard of thee," says he, "by the hearing of the ear, but now mine eye seeth thee; wherefore I abhor myself, and repent in dust and ashes" (Job 42:5,6).

And what mean the tremblings, the tears, those breakings and shakings of heart that attend the people of God, when in an eminent manner they receive the pronunciation of the forgiveness of sins at his mouth, but that the dread of the majesty of God is in their sight mixed therewith? God must appear like himself, speak to the soul like himself; nor can the sinner, when under these glorious discoveries of his Lord and Saviour, keep out the beams of his majesty from the eyes of his understanding. "I will cleanse them," saith he, "from all their iniquity, whereby they have sinned against me, and I will pardon all their iniquities whereby they have sinned, and whereby they have transgressed against me." And what then? "And they shall fear and tremble for all the goodness, and for all the prosperity that I procure unto it" (Jer 33:8,9). Alas! there is a company of poor, light, frothy professors in the world, that carry it under that which they call the presence of God, more like to antics, than sober sensible Christians; yea, more like to a fool of a play, than those that have the presence of God. They would not carry it so in the presence of a king, nor yet of the lord of their land, were they but receivers of mercy at his hand. They carry it even in their most eminent seasons, as if the sense and sight of God, and his blessed grace to their souls in Christ, had a tendency in them to make men wanton: but indeed it is the most humbling and heart-breaking sight in the world; it is fearful.

Object. But would you not have us rejoice at the sight and sense of the forgiveness of our sins?

Answ. Yes; but yet I would have you, and indeed you shall, when God shall tell you that your sins are pardoned indeed, "rejoice with trembling" (Psa 2:11). For then you have solid and godly joy; a joyful heart, and wet eyes, in this will stand very well together; and it will be so more or less. For if God shall come to you indeed, and visit you with the forgiveness of sins, that visit removeth the guilt, but increaseth the sense of thy filth, and the sense of this that God hath forgiven a filthy sinner, will make thee both rejoice and tremble. O, the blessed confusion that will then cover thy face whilst thou, even thou, so vile a wretch, shalt stand before God to receive at his hand thy pardon, and so the firstfruits of thy eternal salvation–"That thou mayest remember, and be confounded, and never open thy mouth any more because of thy shame (thy filth), when I am pacified toward thee for all that thou hast done, saith the Lord God" (Eze 16:63). But,

Second. As the presence, so the name of God, is dreadful and fearful: wherefore his name doth rightly go under the same title, "That thou mayest fear this glorious and fearful name, THE LORD THY GOD" (Deut 28:58). The name of God, what is that, but that by which he is distinguished and known from all others? Names are to distinguish by; so man is distinguished from beasts, and angels from men; so heaven from earth, and darkness from light; especially when by the name, the nature of the thing is signified and expressed; and so it was in their original, for then names expressed the nature of the thing so named. And therefore it is that the name of God is the object of our fear, because by his name his nature is expressed: "Holy and reverend is his name" (Psa 111:9). And again, he proclaimed the name of the Lord, "The Lord, the Lord God, merciful and gracious, long-suffering, and abundant in goodness and truth; keeping mercy for thousands, forgiving iniquity, and transgression, and sin, and that will by no means clear the guilty" (Exo 34:6,7).

Also his name, I am, Jah, Jehovah, with several others, what is by them intended but his nature, as his power, wisdom, eternity, goodness, and omnipotency, &c., might be expressed and declared. The name of God is therefore the object of a Christian's fear. David prayed to God that he would unite his heart to fear his name (Psa 86:11). Indeed, the name of God is a fearful name, and should always be reverenced by his people: yea his "name is to be feared for ever and ever," and that not only in his church, and among his saints, but even in the world and among the heathen–"So the heathen shall fear the name of the Lord, and all kings thy glory" (Psa 102:15). God tells us that his name is dreadful, and that he is pleased to see men be afraid before his name. Yea, one reason why he executeth so many judgments upon men as he doth, is that others might see and fear his name. "So shall they fear the name of the Lord from the west, and his glory from the rising of the sun" (Isa 59:19; Mal 2:5).

The name of a king is a name of fear–"And I am a great king, saith the Lord of hosts" (Mal 1:14). The name of master is a name of fear–"And if I be a master, where is my fear? saith the Lord" (v 6). Yea, rightly to fear the Lord is a sign of a gracious heart. And again, "To you that fear my name," saith he, "shall the Sun of righteousness arise with healing in his wings" (Mal 4:2). Yea, when Christ comes to judge the world, he will give reward to his servants the prophets, and to his saints, "and to them that fear his name, small and great" (Rev 11:18). Now, I say, since the name of God is that by which his nature is expressed, and since he naturally is so glorious and incomprehensible, his name must needs be the object of our fear, and we ought always to have a reverent awe of God upon our hearts at what time soever we think of, or hear his name, but most of all, when we ourselves do take his holy and fearful name into our mouths, especially in a religious manner, that is, in preaching, praying, or holy conference. I do not by thus saying intend as if it was lawful to make mention of his name in light and vain discourses; for we ought always to speak of it with reverence and godly fear, but I speak it to put Christians in mind that they should not in religious duties show lightness of mind, or be vain in their words when yet they are making mention of the name of the Lord–"Let every one that nameth the name of Christ depart from iniquity" (2 Tim 2:19).

Make mention then of the name of the Lord at all times with great dread of his majesty upon our hearts, and in great soberness and truth. To do otherwise is to profane the name of the Lord, and to take his name in vain; and "the Lord will not hold him guiltless that taketh his name in vain." Yea, God saith that he will cut off the man that doth it; so jealous is he of the honour due unto his name (Exo 20:7; Lev 20:3). This therefore showeth you the dreadful state of those that lightly, vainly, lyingly, and profanely make use of the name, this fearful name of God, either by their blasphemous cursing and oaths, or by their fraudulent dealing with their neighbour; for some men have no way to prevail with their neighbour to bow under a cheat, but by calling falsely upon the name of the Lord to be witness that the wickedness is good and honest; but how these men will escape, when they shall be judged, devouring fire and everlasting burnings, for their profaning and blaspheming of the name of the Lord, becomes them betimes to consider of (Jer 14:14,15; Eze 20:39; Exo 20:7).

But,

Third. As the presence and name of God are dreadful and fearful in the church, so is his worship and service. I say his worship, or the works of service to which we are by him enjoined while we are in this world, are dreadful and fearful things. This David conceiveth, when he saith, "But as for me, I will come into thy house in the multitude of thy mercy, and in thy fear will I worship toward thy holy temple" (Psa 5:7). And again, saith he, "Serve the Lord with fear." To praise God is a part of his worship. But, says Moses, "Who is a God like unto thee, glorious in holiness, fearful in praises, doing wonders?" (Exo 15:11). To rejoice before him is a part of his worship; but David bids us "rejoice with trembling" (Psa 2:11). Yea, the whole of our service to God, and every part thereof, ought to be done by us with reverence and godly fear. And therefore let us, as Paul saith again, "Cleanse ourselves from all filthiness of the flesh and spirit, perfecting holiness in the fear of God" (2 Cor 7:1; Heb 12).

1. That which makes the worship of God so fearful a thing, is, for that it is the worship of GOD: all manner of service carries more or less dread and fear along with it, according as the quality or condition of the person is to whom the worship and service is done. This is seen in the service of subjects to their princes, the service of servants to their lords, and the service of children to their parents. Divine worship, then, being due to God, for it is now of Divine worship we speak, and this God so great and dreadful in himself and name, his worship must therefore be a fearful thing.

2. Besides, this glorious Majesty is himself present to behold his worshippers in their worshipping him. "When two or three of you are gathered together in my name, I am there." That is, gathered together to worship him, "I am there," says he. And so, again, he is said to walk "in the midst of the seven golden candlesticks" (Rev 1:13). That is, in the churches, and that with a countenance like the sun, with a head and hair as white as snow, and with eyes like a flame of fire. This puts dread and fear into his service; and therefore his servants should serve him with fear.

3. Above all things, God is jealous of his worship and service. In all the ten words, he telleth us not anything of his being a jealous God, but in the second, which respecteth his worship (Exo 20). Look to yourselves therefore, both as to the matter and manner of your worship; "for I the Lord thy God," says he, "am a jealous God, visiting the iniquity of the fathers upon the children." This therefore doth also put dread and fear into the worship and service of God.

4. The judgments that sometimes God hath executed upon men for their want of godly fear, while they have been in his worship and service, put fear and dread upon his holy appointments. (1.) Nadab and Abihu were burned to death with fire from heaven, because they attempted to offer false fire upon God's altar, and the reason rendered why they were so served, was, because God will be sanctified in them that come nigh him (Lev 10:1-3). To sanctify his name is to let him be thy dread and thy fear, and to do nothing in his worship but what is well-pleasing to him. But because these men had not grace to do this, therefore they died before the Lord. (2.) Eli's sons, for want of this fear, when they ministered in the holy worship of God, were both slain in one day by the sword of the uncircumcised Philistines (see 1 Sam 2). (3.) Uzzah was smitten, and died before the Lord, for but an unadvised touching of the ark, when the men forsook it (1 Chron 13:9,10). (4.) Ananias and Sapphira his wife, for telling a lie in the church, when they were before God, were both stricken dead upon the place before them all, because they wanted the fear and dread of God's majesty, name, and service, when they

came before him (Acts 5).

This therefore should teach us to conclude, that, next to God's nature and name, his service, his instituted worship, is the most dreadful thing under heaven. His name is upon his ordinances, his eye is upon the worshippers, and his wrath and judgment upon those that worship not in his fear. For this cause some of those at Corinth were by God himself cut off, and to others he has given the back, and will again be with them no more (1 Cor 11:27-32).

This also rebuketh three sorts of people.

[Three sorts of people rebuked.]

1. Such as regard not to worship God at all; be sure they have no reverence of his service, nor fear of his majesty before their eyes. Sinner, thou dost not come before the Lord to worship him; thou dost not bow before the high God; thou neither worshippest him in thy closet nor in the congregation of saints. The fury of the Lord and his indignation must in short time be poured out upon thee, and upon the families that call not upon his name (Psa 79:6; Jer 10:25).

2. This rebukes such as count it enough to present their body in the place where God is worshipped, not minding with what heart, or with what spirit they come thither. Some come into the worship of God to sleep there; some come thither to meet with their chapmen, and to get into the wicked fellowship of their vain companions. Some come thither to feed their lustful and adulterous eyes with the flattering beauty of their fellow-sinners. O what a sad account will these worshippers give, when they shall count for all this, and be damned for it, because they come not to worship the Lord with that fear of his name that became them to come in, when they presented themselves before him!

3. This also rebukes those that care not, so they worship, how they worship; how, where, or after what manner they worship God. Those, I mean, whose fear towards God "is taught by the precept of men." They are hypocrites; their worship also is vain, and a stink in the nostrils of God. "Wherefore the Lord said, Forasmuch as this people draw near me with their mouth, and with their lips do honour me, but have removed their heart far from me, and their fear toward me is taught by the precept of men: therefore, behold I will proceed to do a marvellous work among this people, even a marvellous work and a wonder: for the wisdom of their wise men shall perish, and the understanding of their prudent men shall be hid" (Isa 29:13,14; Matt 15:7-9; Mark 7:6,7). Thus I conclude this first thing, namely, that God is called our

dread and fear.

OF THIS WORD FEAR AS IT IS TAKEN FOR THE WORD OF GOD.

I shall now come to the second thing, to wit, to the rule and director of our fear.

SECOND. But again, this word FEAR is sometimes to be taken for THE WORD, the written Word of God; for that also is, and ought to be, the rule and director of our fear. So David calls it in the nineteenth Psalm: "the fear of the Lord," saith he, "is clean, enduring for ever." The fear of the Lord, that is, the Word of the Lord, the written word; for that which he calleth in this place the fear of the Lord, even in the same place he calleth the law, statutes, commandments, and judgments of God. "The law of the Lord is perfect, converting the soul: the testimony of the Lord is sure, making wise the simple: the statutes of the Lord are right, rejoicing the heart: the commandment of the Lord is pure, enlightening the eyes: the fear of the Lord is clean, enduring for ever: the judgments of the Lord are true and righteous altogether." All these words have respect to the same thing, to wit, to the Word of God, jointly designing the glory of it. Among which phrases, as you see, this is one, "The fear of the Lord is clean, enduring for ever." This written Word is therefore the object of a Christian's fear. This is that also which David intended when he said, "Come, ye children, hearken unto me, I will teach you the fear of the Lord" (Psa 34:11). I will teach you the fear, that is, I will teach you the commandments, statutes, and judgments of the Lord, even as Moses commanded the children of Israel—"Thou shalt teach them diligently unto thy children, and shalt talk of them when thou sittest in thine house, and when thou walkest by the way, and when thou liest down, and when thou risest up" (Deut 6:4-7).

That also in the eleventh of Isaiah intends the same, where the Father saith of the Son, that he shall be of quick understanding in the fear of the Lord; that he may judge and smite the earth with the rod of his mouth. This rod in the text is none other but the fear, the Word of the Lord; for he was to be of a quick understanding, that he might smite, that is, execute it according to the will of his Father, upon and among the children of men. Now this, as I said, is called the fear of the Lord, because it is called the rule and director of our fear. For we know not how to fear the Lord in a saving way without its guidance and direction. As it is said of the priest that was sent back from the captivity to Samaria to teach the people to fear the Lord, so it is said concerning the written Word; it is given to us, and left among us, that we may read therein all the days of our life, and learn to fear the Lord (Deut 6:1-3,24, 10:12, 17:19). And here it is that, trembling at the Word of God, is even by God himself not only taken notice of, but counted as laudable and praiseworthy, as is evident in the case of Josiah (2 Chron 34:26,27). Such also are the approved of God, let them be condemned by whomsoever: "Hear the word of the Lord, ye that tremble at his word; Your brethren that hated you, that cast you out for my name's sake, said, Let the Lord be glorified; but he shall appear to your joy, and they shall be ashamed" (Isa 66:5).

Further, such shall be looked to, by God himself cared for, and watched over, that no distress, temptation, or affliction may overcome them and destroy them—"To this man will I look," saith God, "even to him that is poor and of a contrite spirit, and that trembleth at my word." It is the same in substance with that in the same prophet in chapter 57: "For thus saith the high and lofty One that inhabiteth eternity, whose name is Holy; I dwell in the high and holy place, with him also that is of a contrite and humble spirit, to revive the spirit of the humble, and to revive the heart of the contrite ones." Yea, the way to escape dangers foretold, is to hearken to, understand, and fear the Word of God—"He that feared the word of the Lord among the servants of Pharaoh, made his servants and his cattle flee into the houses," and they were secured; but "he that regarded not the word of the Lord, left his servants and his cattle in the field," and they were destroyed of the hail (Exo 9:20-25).

If at any time the sins of a nation or church are discovered and bewailed, it is by them that know and tremble at the word of God. When Ezra heard of the wickedness of his brethren, and had a desire to humble himself before God for the same, who were they that would assist him in that matter, but they that trembled at the word of God?—"Then," saith he, "were assembled unto me every one that trembled at the words of the God of Israel, because of the transgression of those that had been carried away" (Ezra 9:4). They are such also that tremble at the Word that are best able to give counsel in the matters of God, for their judgment best suiteth with his mind and will: "Now therefore," said he, "let us make a covenant with our God to put away all the (strange) wives, - according to the counsel of my Lord, and of those that tremble at the commandment of our God, and let it be done according to the law" (Ezra 10:3). Now something of the dread and terror of the Word lieth in these things.

First. As I have already hinted, from the author of them, they are the words of God. Therefore you have Moses and the prophets, when they came to deliver their errand, their message to the people, still saying, "Hear the word of the Lord," "Thus saith the Lord," and the like. So when Ezekiel was sent to the house of Israel, in their state of religion, thus was he bid to say unto them, "Thus saith the Lord God" ; "Thus saith the Lord God" (Eze 2:4, 3:11). This is the honour and majesty, then, that God hath put upon his written Word, and thus he hath done even of purpose, that we might make them the rule and directory of our fear, and that we might stand in awe of, and tremble at them. When Habakkuk heard the word of the Lord, his belly trembled, and rottenness entered into his bones. "I trembled in myself," said he, "that I might rest in the day of trouble" (Hab 3:16). The word of a king is as the roaring of a lion; where the word of a king is, there is power. What is it, then, when God, the great God, shall roar out of Zion, and utter his voice from Jerusalem, whose voice shakes not only the earth, but also heaven? How doth holy David set it forth; "The voice of the Lord is powerful, the voice of the Lord is full of majesty," &c. (Psa 29).

Second. It is a Word that is fearful, and may well be called the fear of the Lord, because of the subject matter of it; to wit, the state of sinners in another world; for that is it unto which the whole Bible bendeth itself, either more immediately or more mediately. All its doctrines, counsels, encouragements, threatenings, and judgments, have a look, one way or other, upon us, with respect to the next world, which will be our last state, because it will be to us a state eternal. This word, this law, these judgments, are they that we shall be disposed of by—"The word that I have spoken," says Christ, "it shall judge you (and so consequently dispose of you) in the last day" (John 12:48). Now, if we consider that our next state must be eternal, either eternal glory or eternal fire, and that this eternal glory or this eternal fire must be our portion, according as the words of God, revealed in the holy Scriptures, shall determine; who will not but conclude that therefore the words of God are they at which we should tremble, and they by which we should have our fear of God guided and directed, for by them we are taught how to please him in everything?

Third. It is to be called a fearful Word, because of the truth and faithfulness of it. The Scriptures cannot be broken. Here they are called the Scriptures of truth, the true sayings of God, and also the fear of the Lord, for that every jot and tittle thereof is for ever settled in heaven, and stand more steadfast than doth the world—"Heaven and earth," saith Christ, "shall pass away, but my words shall not pass away" (Matt 24:35). Those, therefore, that are favoured by the Word of God, those are favoured indeed, and that with the favour that no man can turn away; but those that by the word of the Scriptures are condemned, those can no man justify and set quit in the sight of God. Therefore what is bound by the text, is bound, and what is released by the text, is released; also the bond and release is unalterable (Dan 10:21; Rev 19:9; Matt 24:35; Psa 119:89; John 10:35). This, therefore, calleth upon God's people to stand more in fear of the Word of God than of all the terrors of the world. There wanteth even in the hearts of God's people a greater reverence of the Word of God than to this day appeareth among us, and this let me say, that want of reverence of the Word is the ground of all disorders that are in the heart, life, conversation, and in Christian communion. Besides, the want of reverence of the Word layeth men open to the fearful displeasure of God—"Whoso despiseth the word shall be destroyed; but he that feareth the commandment shall be rewarded" (Prov 13:13).

All transgression beginneth at wandering from the Word of God; but, on the other side, David saith, "Concerning the works of men, by the word of thy lips I have kept me from the paths of the destroyer" (Psa 17:4). Therefore Solomon saith, "My son, attend to my words; incline thine ear unto my sayings; let them not depart from thine eyes; keep them in the midst of thine heart; for they are life unto those that find them, and health to all their flesh" (Prov 4:20-22). Now, if indeed thou wouldest reverence the Word of the Lord, and make it thy rule and director in all things, believe that the Word is the fear of the Lord, the Word that standeth fast for ever; without and against which God will do nothing, either in saving or damning of the souls of sinners. But to conclude this,

1. Know that those that have no due regard to the Word of the Lord, and that make it not their dread and their fear, but the rule of their life is the lust of their flesh, the desire of their eyes, and the pride of life, are sorely rebuked by this doctrine, and are counted the fools of the world; for "lo, they have rejected the word of the Lord, and what wisdom is in them?" (Jer 8:9). That there are such a people is evident, not only by their irregular lives, but by the manifest testimony of the Word. "As for the word of the Lord," said they to Jeremiah, "that thou hast spoken to us in the name of the Lord, we will not hearken unto thee, but we will certainly do whatsoever thing goeth forth out of our own mouth" (Jer 44:16). Was this only the temper of wicked men then? Is not the same spirit of rebellion amongst us in our days? Doubtless there is; for there is no new thing—"The thing that hath been, it is that which shall be, and that which is done is that which shall be done; and there is no new thing under the sun" (Eccl 1:9). Therefore, as it was then, so it is with many in this day.

As for the Word of the Lord, it is nothing at all to them; their lusts, and whatsoever proceedeth out of their own mouths, that they will do, that they will follow. Now, such will certainly perish in their own rebellion; for this is as the sin of witchcraft; it was the sin of Korah and his company, and that which brought upon them such heavy judgments; yea, and they are made a sign that thou shouldest not do as they, for they perished (because they rejected the word, the fear of the Lord) from among the congregation of the Lord, "and they became a sign." The word which thou despisest still abideth to denounce its woe and judgment upon thee; and unless God will save such with the breath of his word—and it is hard trusting to that—they must never see his face with comfort (1 Sam 15:22,23; Num 26:9,10).

2. Are the words of God called by the name of the fear of the Lord? Are they so dreadful in their receipt and sentence? Then this rebukes them that esteem the words and things of men more than the words of God, as those do who are drawn from their respect of, and obedience to, the Word of God, by the pleasures or threats of men. Some there be who verily will acknowledge the authority of the Word, yet will not stoop their souls thereto. Such, whatever they think of themselves, are judged by Christ to be ashamed of the Word; wherefore their state is damnable as the other. "Whosoever," saith he, "shall be ashamed of me and of my words, in this adulterous and sinful generation, of him also shall the Son of man be ashamed, when he cometh in the glory of the Father, with the holy angels" (Mark 8:38).

3. And if these things be so, what will become of those that mock at, and professedly contemn, the words of God, making them as a thing ridiculous, and not to be regarded? Shall they prosper that do such things? From the promises it is concluded that their judgment now of a long time slumbereth not, and when it comes, it will devour them without remedy (2 Chron 36:15). If God, I say, hath put that reverence upon his Word as to call it the fear of the Lord, what will become of them that do what they can to overthrow its authority, by denying it to be his Word, and by raising cavils against its authority? Such stumble, indeed, at the Word, being appointed thereunto, but it shall judge them in the last day (1 Peter 2:8; John 12:48). But thus much for this.

OF SEVERAL SORTS OF FEAR OF GOD IN THE HEART OF THE CHILDREN OF MEN.

Having thus spoken of the object and rule of our fear, I should come now to speak of fear as it is a grace of the Spirit of God in the hearts of his people; but before I do that, I shall show you that there are divers sorts of fear besides. For man being a reasonable creature, and having even by nature a certain knowledge of God, hath also naturally something of some kind of fear of God at times, which, although it be not that which is intended in the text, yet ought to be spoken to, that that which is not right may be distinguished from that that is.

There is, I say, several sorts or kinds of fear in the hearts of the sons of men, I mean besides that fear of God that is intended in the text, and that accompanieth eternal life. I shall here make mention of three of them. FIRST. There is a fear of God that flows even from the light of nature. SECOND. There is a fear of God that flows from some of his dispensations to men, which yet is neither universal nor saving. THIRD. There is a fear of God in the heart of some men that is good and godly, but doth not for ever abide so. To speak a little to all these, before I come to speak of fear, as it is a grace of God in the hearts of his children, And,

FIRST. To the first, to wit, that there is a fear of God that flows even from the light of nature. A people may be said to do things in a fear of God, when they act one towards another in things reasonable, and honest betwixt man and man, not doing that to others they would not have done to themselves. This is that fear of God which Abraham thought the Philistines had destroyed in themselves, when he said of his wife to Abimelech, "She is my sister." For when Abimelech asked Abraham why he said of his wife, She is my sister; he replied, saying, "I thought surely the fear of God is not in this place, and they will slay me for my wife's sake" (Gen 20:11). I thought verily that in this place men had stifled and choked that light of nature that is in them, at least so far forth as not to suffer it to put them in fear, when their lusts were powerful in them to accomplish their ends on the object that was present before them. But this I will pass by, and come to the second thing, namely—

SECOND. To show that there is a fear of God that flows from some of his dispensations to men, which yet is neither universal nor saving. This fear, when opposed to that which is saving, may be called an ungodly fear of God. I shall describe it by these several particulars that follow—

First. There is a fear of God that causeth a continual grudging, discontent, and heart-risings against God under the hand of God; and that is, when the dread of God in his coming upon men, to deal with them for their sins, is apprehended by them, and yet by this dispensation they have no change of heart to submit to God thereunder. The sinners under this dispensation cannot shake God out of their mind, nor yet graciously tremble before him; but through the unsanctified frame that they now are in, they are afraid with ungodly fear, and so in their minds let fly against him. This fear oftentimes took hold of the children of Israel when they were in the wilderness in their journey to the promised land; still they feared that God in this place would destroy them, but not with that fear that made them willing to submit, for their sins, to the judgment which they fear, but with that fear that made them let fly against God. This fear showed itself in them, even at the beginning of their voyage, and was rebuked by Moses at the Red Sea, but it was not there, nor yet at any other place, so subdued, but that it would rise again in them at times to the dishonour of God, and the anew making of them guilty of sin before him (Exo 14:11-13; Num 14:1-9). This fear is that which God said he would send before them, in the day of Joshua, even a fear that should possess the inhabitants of the land, to wit, a fear that should arise for that faintness of heart that they should be swallowed up of, at their apprehending of Joshua in his approaches towards them to destroy them. "I will send my fear before thee, and will destroy all the people to whom thou shalt come, and I will make all thine enemies turn their backs unto thee" (Exo 23:27). "This day," says God, "will I begin to put the dread of thee, and the fear of thee upon the nations that are under the whole heaven who shall hear report of thee, and shall tremble, and be in anguish because of thee" (Deut 2:25, 11:25).

Now this fear is also, as you here see, called anguish, and in another place, an hornet; for it, and the soul that it falls upon, do greet each other, as boys and bees do. The hornet puts men in fear, not so as to bring the heart into a sweet compliance with his terror, but so as to stir up the spirit into acts of opposition and resistance, yet withal they flee before it. "I will send hornets before thee, which shall drive out the Hivite," &c. (Exo 23:28). Now this fear, whether it be wrought by misapprehending of the judgments of God, as in the Israelites, or otherwise as in the Canaanites, yet ungodliness is the effect thereof, and therefore I call it an ungodly fear of God, for it stirreth up murmurings, discontents, and heart-risings against God, while he with his dispensations is dealing with them.

Second. There is a fear of God that driveth a man away from God—I speak not now of the atheist, nor of the pleasurable sinner, nor yet of these, and that fear that I spoke of just now—I speak now of such who through a sense of sin and of God's justice fly from him of a slavish ungodly fear. This ungodly fear was that which possessed Adam's heart in the day that he did eat of the tree concerning which the Lord has said unto him, "In the day that thou eatest thereof, thou shalt surely die." For then was he possessed with such a fear of God as made him seek to hide himself from his presence. "I heard," said he, "thy voice in the garden, and I was afraid, because I was naked; and I hid myself" (Gen 3:10). Mind it, he had a fear of God, but it was not godly. It was not that that made him afterwards submit himself unto him; for that would have kept him from not departing from him, or else have brought him to him again, with bowed, broken, and contrite spirit. But this fear, as the rest of his sin, managed his departing from his God, and pursued him to provoke him still so to do; by it he kept himself from God, by it his whole man was carried away from him. I call it ungodly fear, because it begat in him ungodly apprehensions of his Maker; because it confined Adam's conscience to the sense of justice only, and consequently to despair.

The same fear also possessed the children of Israel when they heard the law delivered to them on Mount Sinai; as is evident, for it made them that they could neither abide his presence nor hear his word. It drove them back from the mountain. It made them, saith the apostle to the Hebrews, that "they could not endure that which was commanded" (Heb 12:20). Wherefore this fear Moses rebukes, and forbids their giving way thereto. "Fear not," said he; but had that fear been godly, he would have encouraged it, and not forbid and rebuke it as he did. "Fear not," said he, "for God is come to prove you"; they thought otherwise. "God," saith he, "is come to prove you, and that his fear may be before your faces." Therefore that fear that already had taken possession of them, was not the fear of God, but a fear that was of Satan, of their own misjudging hearts, and so a fear that was ungodly (Exo 20:18-20). Mark you, here is a fear and a fear, a fear forbidden, and a fear commended; a fear forbidden, because it engendered their hearts to bondage, and to ungodly thoughts of God and of his word; it made them that they could not desire to hear God speak to them any more (vv 19-21).

Many also at this day are possessed with this ungodly fear; and you may know them by this,—they cannot abide conviction for sin, and if at any time the word of the law, by the preaching of the word, comes near them, they will not abide that preacher, nor such kind of sermons any more. They are, as they deem, best at ease, when furthest off of God, and of the power of his word. The word preached brings God nearer to them than they desire he should come, because whenever God comes near, their sins by him are manifest, and so is the judgment too that to them is due. Now these not having faith in the mercy of God through Christ, nor that grace that tendeth to bring them to him, they cannot but think of God amiss, and their so thinking of him makes them say unto him, "Depart from us, for we desire not the knowledge of thy ways" (Job 21:14). Wherefore their wrong thoughts of

God beget in them this ungodly fear; and again, this ungodly fear doth maintain in them the continuance of these wrong and unworthy thoughts of God, and therefore, through that devilish service wherewith they strengthen one another, the sinner, without a miracle of grace prevents him, is drowned in destruction and perdition.

It was this ungodly fear of God that carried Cain from the presence of God into the land of Nod, and that put him there upon any carnal worldly business, if perhaps he might by so doing stifle convictions of the majesty and justice of God against his sin, and so live the rest of his vain life in the more sinful security and fleshly ease. This ungodly fear is that also which Samuel perceived at the people's apprehension of their sin, to begin to get hold of their hearts; wherefore he, as Moses before him, quickly forbids their entertaining of it. "Fear not," said he, "ye have done all this wickedness, yet turn not aside from following the Lord." For to turn them aside from following of him, was the natural tendency of this fear. "But fear not," said he, that is, with that fear that tendeth to turn you aside. Now, I say, the matter that this fear worketh upon, as in Adam, and the Israelites mentioned before, was their sin. You have sinned, says he, that is true, yet turn not aside, yet fear not with that fear that would make you so do (1 Sam 12:20). Note by the way, sinner, that when the greatness of thy sins, being apprehended by thee, shall work in thee that fear of God, as shall incline thy heart to fly from him, thou art possessed with a fear of God that is ungodly, yea, so ungodly, that not any of thy sins for heinousness may be compared therewith, as might be made manifest in many particulars, but Samuel having rebuked this fear, presently sets before the people another, to wit, the true fear of God; "fear the Lord," says he, "serve him - with all your heart" (v 24). And he giveth them this encouragement so to do, "for the Lord will not forsake his people." This ungodly fear is that which you read of in Isaiah 2, and in many other places, and God's people should shun it, as they would shun the devil, because its natural tendency is to forward the destruction of the soul in which it has taken possession.

Third. There is a fear of God, which, although it hath not in it that power as to make men flee from God's presence, yet it is ungodly, because, even while they are in the outward way of God's ordinances, their hearts are by it quite discouraged from attempting to exercise themselves in the power of religion. Of this sort are they which dare not cast off the hearing, reading, and discourse of the word as others; no, nor the assembly of God's children for the exercise of other religious duties, for their conscience is convinced this is the way and worship of God. But yet their heart, as I said, by this ungodly fear, is kept from a powerful gracious falling in with God. This fear takes away their heart from all holy and godly prayer in private, and from all holy and godly zeal for his name in public, and there be many professors whose hearts are possessed with this ungodly fear of God; and they are intended by the slothful one. He was a servant, a servant among the servants of God, and had gifts and abilities given him, therewith to serve Christ, as well as his fellows, yea, and was commanded too, as well as the rest, to occupy till his master came. But what does he? Why, he takes his talent, the gift that he was to lay out for his master's profit, and puts it in a napkin, digs a hole in the earth, and hides his lord's money, and lies in a lazy manner at to-elbow all his days, not out of, but in his lord's vineyard; for he came among the servants also at last. By which it is manifest that he had not cast off his profession, but was slothful and negligent while he was in it. But what was it that made him thus slothful?

What was it that took away his heart, while he was in the way, and that discouraged him from falling in with the power and holy practice of religion according to the talent he received? Why, it was this, he gave way to an ungodly fear of God, and that took away his heart from the power of religious duties. "Lord," said he, "behold, here is thy pound, which I have kept, laid up in a napkin, for I feared thee." Why, man, doth the fear of God make a man idle and slothful? No, no; that is, if it be right and godly. This fear was therefore evil fear; it was that ungodly fear of God which I have here been speaking of. For I feared thee, or as Matthew hath it, "for I was afraid." Afraid of what? Of Christ, "that he was an hard man, reaping where he sowed not, and gathering where he had not strawed." This his fear, being ungodly, made him apprehend of Christ contrary to the goodness of his nature, and so took away his heart from all endeavours to be doing of that which was pleasing in his sight (Luke 19:20; Matt 25:24, 25). And thus do all those that retain the name and show of religion, but are neglecters as to the power and godly practice of it. These will live like dogs and swine in the house; they pray not, they watch not their hearts, they pull not their hands out of their bosoms to work, they do not strive against their lusts, nor will they ever resist unto blood, striving against sin; they cannot take up their cross, or improve what they have to God's glory. Let all men therefore take heed of this ungodly fear, and shun it as they shun the devil, for it will make them afraid where no fear is. It will tell them that there is a lion in the street, the unlikeliest place in the world for such a beast to be in; it will put a vizard upon the face of God, most dreadful and fearful to behold, and then quite discourage the soul as to his service; so it served the slothful servant, and so it will serve thee, poor sinner, if thou entertainest it, and givest way thereto. But,

Fourth. This ungodly fear of God shows itself also in this. It will not suffer the soul that is governed thereby to trust only to Christ for justification of life, but will bend the powers of the soul to trust partly to the works of the law. Many of the Jews were, in the time of Christ and his apostles, possessed with this ungodly fear of God, for they were not as the former, to wit, as the slothful servant, to receive a talent and hide it in the earth in a napkin, but they were an industrious people, they followed after the law of righteousness, they had a zeal of God and of the religion of their fathers; but how then did they come to miscarry? Why, their fear of God was ungodly; it would not suffer them wholly to trust to the righteousness of faith, which is the imputed righteousness of Christ. They followed after the law of righteousness, but attained not to the law of righteousness. Wherefore? because they sought it not by faith, but as it were by the works of the law. But what was it that made them join their works of the law with Christ, but their unbelief, whose foundation was ignorance and fear? They were afraid to venture all in one bottom, they thought two strings to one bow would be best, and thus betwixt two stools they came to the ground. And hence, to fear and to doubt, are put together as being the cause one of another; yea, they are put ofttimes the one for the other; thus ungodly fear for unbelief: "Be not afraid, only believe," and therefore he that is overruled and carried away with this fear, is coupled with the unbeliever that is thrust out from the holy city among the dogs. But the fearful and unbelievers, and murderers are without (Rev 21:8). "The fearful and unbelieving," you see, are put together; for indeed fear, that is, this ungodly fear, is the ground of unbelief, or, if you will, unbelief is the ground of fear, this fear: but I stand not upon nice distinctions. This ungodly fear hath a great hand in keeping of the soul from trusting only to Christ's righteousness for justification of life.

Fifth. This ungodly fear of God is that which will put men upon adding to the revealed will of God their own inventions, and their own performances of them, as a means to pacify the anger of God. For the truth is, where this ungodly fear reigneth, there is no end of law and duty. When those that you read of in the book of Kings were destroyed by the lions, because they had set up idolatry in the land of Israel, they sent for a priest from Babylon that might teach them the manner of the God of the land; but behold when they knew it, being taught it by the priest, yet their fear would not suffer them to be content with that worship only. "They feared the Lord," saith the text, "and served their own gods." And again, "So these nations feared the Lord, and served their graven images" (2 Kings 17). It was this fear also that put the Pharisees upon inventing so many traditions, as the washing of cups, and beds, and tables, and basins, with abundance of such other like gear, none knows the many dangers that an ungodly fear of God will drive a man into (Mark 7). How has it racked and tortured the Papists for hundreds of years together! for what else is the cause but this ungodly fear, at least in the most simple and harmless of them, of their penances, as creeping to the cross, going barefoot on pilgrimage, whipping themselves, wearing of sackcloth, saying so many Pater-nosters, so many Ave- marias, making so many confessions to the priest, giving so much money for pardons, and abundance of other the like, but this ungodly fear of God? For could they be brought to believe this doctrine, that Christ was delivered for our offences, and raised again for our justification, and to apply it by faith with godly boldness to their own souls, this fear would vanish, and so consequently all those things with which they so needlessly and unprofitably afflicted themselves, offend God, and grieve his people. Therefore, gentle reader, although my text doth bid that indeed thou shouldest fear God, yet it includeth not, nor accepteth of any fear; no, not of any [or every] fear of God. For there is, as you see, a fear of God that is ungodly, and that is to be shunned as their sin. Wherefore thy wisdom and thy care should be, to see and prove thy fear to be godly, which shall be the next thing that I shall take in hand.

THIRD. The third thing that I am to speak to is, that there is a fear of God in the heart of some men that is good and godly, but yet doth not for ever abide so. Or you may take it thus—There is a fear of God that is godly but for a time. In my speaking to, and opening of this to you, I shall observe this method. First. I shall show you what this fear is. Second. I shall show you by whom or what this fear is wrought in the heart. Third. I shall show you what this fear doth in the soul. And, Fourth, I shall show you when this fear is to have an end.

First. For the first, this fear is an effect of sound awakenings by the word of wrath which begetteth in the soul a sense of its right to eternal damnation; for this fear is not in every sinner; he that is blinded by the devil, and that is not able to see that his state is damnable, he hath not this fear in his heart, but he that is under the powerful workings of the word of wrath, as God's elect are at first conversion, he hath this godly fear in his heart; that is, he fears that that damnation will come upon him, which by the justice of God is due unto him, because he hath broken his holy law. This is the fear that made the three thousand cry out, "Men and brethren, what shall we do?" and that made the jailer cry out, and that with great trembling of soul, "Sirs, what must I do to be saved?" (Acts 2, 16). The method of God is to kill and make alive, to smite and then heal; when the commandment came to Paul, sin revived, and he died, and that law which was ordained to life, he found to be unto death; that is, it passed a sentence of death upon him for his sins, and slew his conscience with that sentence. Therefore from that time that he heard that word, "Why persecutest thou me?" which is all one as if he had said, Why dost thou commit murder? he lay under the sentence of condemnation by the law, and under this fear of that sentence in his conscience. He lay, I say, under it, until that Ananias came to him to comfort him, and to preach unto him the forgiveness of sin (Acts 9). The fear therefore that now I call godly, it is that fear which is properly called the fear of eternal damnation for sin, and this fear, at first awakening, is good and godly, because it ariseth in the soul from a true sense of its very state. Its state by nature is damnable, because it is sinful, and because he is not one that as yet believeth in Christ for remission of sins: "He that believeth not shall be damned."—"He that believeth not is condemned already, and the wrath of God abideth on him" (Mark 16:16; John 3:18,36). The which when the sinner at first begins to see, he justly fears it; I say, he fears it justly, and therefore godly, because by this fear he subscribes to the sentence that is gone out against him for sin.

Second. By whom or by what is this fear wrought in the heart? To this I shall answer in brief. It is wrought in the heart by the Spirit of God, working there at first as a spirit of bondage, on purpose to put us in fear. This Paul insinuateth, saying, "Ye have not received the spirit of bondage again to fear" (Rom 8:15). He doth not say, Ye have not received the spirit of bondage; for that they had received, and that to put them in fear, which was at their first conversion, as by the instances made mention of before is manifest; all that he says is, that they had not received it again, that is, after the Spirit, as a spirit of adoption, is come; for then, as a spirit of bondage, it cometh no more. It is then the Spirit of God, even the Holy Ghost, that convinceth us of sin, and so of our damnable state because of sin (John 16:8,9). For it cannot be that the Spirit of God should convince us of sin, but it must also show us our state to be damnable because of it, especially if it so convinceth us, before we believe, and that is the intent of our Lord in that place, "of sin," and so of their damnable state by sin, because they believe not on me. Therefore the Spirit of God, when he worketh in the heart as a spirit of bondage, he doth it by working in us by the law, "for by the law is the knowledge of sin" (Rom 3:20). And he, in this his working, is properly called a spirit of bondage.

1. Because by the law he shows us that indeed we are in bondage to the law, the devil, and death and damnation; for this is our proper state by nature, though we see it not until the Spirit of God shall come to reveal this our state of bondage unto our own senses by revealing to us our sins by the law.

2. He is called, in this his working, "the spirit of bondage," because he here also holds us; to wit, in this sight and sense of our bondage-state, so long as is meet we should be so held, which to some of the saints is a longer, and to some a shorter time. Paul was held in it three days and three nights, but the jailer and the three thousand, so far as can be gathered, not above an hour; but some in these later times are so held for days and months, if not years. But, I say, let the time be longer or shorter, it is the Spirit of God that holdeth

him under this yoke; and it is good that a man should be in HIS time held under it, as is that saying of the lamentation, "It is good for a man that he bear the yoke in his youth" (Lam 3:27). That is, at his first awakening; so long as seems good to this Holy Spirit to work in this manner by the law. Now, as I said, the sinner at first is by the Spirit of God held in this bondage, that is, hath such a discovery of his sin and of his damnation for sin made to him, and also is held so fast under the sense thereof, that it is not in the power of any man, nor yet of the very angels in heaven, to release him or set him free, until the Holy Spirit changeth his ministration, and comes in the sweet and peaceable tidings of salvation by Christ in the gospel to his poor, dejected, and afflicted conscience.

Third. I now come to show you what this fear doth in the soul. Now, although this godly fear is not to last always with us, as I shall further show you anon, yet it greatly differs from that which is wholly ungodly of itself, both because of the author, and also of the effects of it. Of the author I have told you before; I now shall tell you what it doth.

1. This fear makes a man judge himself for sin, and to fall down before God with a broken mind under this judgment; the which is pleasing to God, because the sinner by so doing justifies God in his saying, and clears him in his judgment (Psa 51:1-4).

2. As this fear makes a man judge himself, and cast himself down at God's foot, so it makes him condole and bewail his misery before him, which is also well-pleasing in his sight: "I have surely heard Ephraim bemoaning himself," saying, "Thou hast chastised me, and I was chastised, as a bullock unaccustomed to the yoke," &c. (Jer 31:18,19).

3. This fear makes a man lie at God's foot, and puts his mouth in the dust, if so be there may be hope. This also is well-pleasing to God, because now is the sinner as nothing, and in his own eyes less than nothing, as to any good or desert: "He sitteth alone and keepeth silence," because he hath now this yoke upon him; "he putteth his mouth in the dust, if so be there may be hope" (Lam 3:28,29).

4. This fear puts a man upon crying to God for mercy, and that in most humble manner; now he sensibly cries, now he dejectedly cries, now he feels and cries, now he smarts and criest out, "God be merciful to me a sinner" (Luke 18:13).

5. This fear makes a man that he cannot accept of that for support and succour which others that are destitute thereof will take up, and be contented

with. This man must be washed by God himself, and cleansed from his sin by God himself (Psa 51).

6. Therefore this fear goes not away until the Spirit of God doth change his ministration as to this particular, in leaving off to work now by the law, as afore, and coming to the soul with the sweet word of promise of life and salvation by Jesus Christ. Thus far this fear is godly, that is, until Christ by the Spirit in the gospel is revealed and made over unto us, and no longer.

Thus far this fear is godly, and the reason why it is godly is because the groundwork of it is good. I told you before what this fear is; namely, it is the fear of damnation. Now the ground for this fear is good, as is manifest by these particulars. 1. The soul feareth damnation, and that rightly, because it is in its sins. 2. The soul feareth damnation rightly, because it hath not faith in Christ, but is at present under the law. 3. The soul feareth damnation rightly now, because by sin, the law, and for want of faith, the wrath of God abideth on it. But now, although thus far this fear of God is good and godly, yet after Christ by the Spirit in the word of the gospel is revealed to us, and we made to accept of him as so revealed and offered to us by a true and living faith; this fear, to wit, of damnation, is no longer good, but ungodly. Nor doth the Spirit of God ever work it in us again. Now we do not receive the spirit of bondage again to fear, that is to say, to fear damnation, but we have received the spirit of adoption, whereby we cry, Father, Father. But I would not be mistaken, when I say, that this fear is no longer godly. I do not mean with reference to the essence and habit of it, for I believe it is the same in the seed which shall afterwards grow up to a higher degree, and into a more sweet and gospel current and manner of working, but I mean reference to this act of fearing damnation, I say it shall never by the Spirit be managed to that work; it shall never bring forth that fruit more. And my reasons are,

Reasons why the Spirit of God cannot work this ungodly fear.

1. Because that the soul by closing through the promise, by the Spirit, with Jesus Christ, is removed off of that foundation upon which it stood when it justly feared damnation. It hath received now forgiveness of sin, it is now no more under the law, but in Jesus Christ by faith; there is "therefore now no condemnation to it" (Acts 26:18; Rom 6:14, 8:1). The groundwork, therefore, being now taken away, the Spirit worketh that fear no more.

2. He cannot, after he hath come to the soul as a spirit of adoption, come again as a spirit of bondage to put the soul into his first fear; to wit, a fear of eternal damnation, because he cannot say and unsay, do and undo. As a spirit of adoption he told me that my sins were forgiven me, that I was included in the covenant of grace, that God was my Father through Christ, that I was under the promise of salvation, and that this calling and gift of God to me is permanent, and without repentance. And do you think, that after he hath told me this, and sealed up the truth of it to my precious soul, that he will come to me, and tell me that I am yet in my sins, under the curse of the law and the eternal wrath of God? No, no, the word of the gospel is not yea, yea; nay, nay. It is only yea, and amen; it is so, "as God is true" (2 Cor 1:17-20).

3. The state therefore of the sinner being changed, and that, too, by the Spirit's changing his dispensation, leaving off to be now as a spirit of bondage to put us in fear, and coming to our heart as the spirit of adoption to make us cry, Father, Father, he cannot go back to his first work again; for if so, then he must gratify, yea, and also ratify, that profane and popish doctrine, forgiven to-day, unforgiven to-morrow—a child of God to-day, a child of hell to-morrow; but what saith the Scriptures? "Now therefore ye are no more strangers and foreigners, but fellow-citizens with the saints, and of the household of God; and are built upon the foundation of the apostles and prophets, Jesus Christ himself being the chief corner stone; in whom all the building fitly framed together groweth unto an holy temple in the Lord; in whom ye also are builded together for an habitation of God through the Spirit" (Eph 2:19-22).

Object. But this is contrary to my experience. Why, Christian, what is thy experience? Why, I was at first, as you have said, possessed with a fear of damnation, and so under the power of the spirit of bondage. Well said, and how was it then? Why, after some time of continuance in these fears, I had the spirit of adoption sent to me to seal up to my soul the forgiveness of sins, and so he did; and was also helped by the same Spirit, as you have said, to call God Father, Father. Well said, and what after that? Why, after that I fell into as great fears as ever I was in before.

Answ. All this may be granted, and yet nevertheless what I have said will abide a truth; for I have not said that after the spirit of adoption is come, a Christian shall not again be in as great fears, for he may have worse than he had at first; but I say, that after the spirit of adoption is come, the spirit of bondage, as such, is sent of God no more, to put us into those fears. For, mark, for we "have not received the spirit of bondage again to fear." Let the word be true, whatever thy experience is. Dost thou not understand me?

After the Spirit of God has told me, and also helped me to believe it, that the Lord for Christ's sake hath forgiven mine iniquities: he tells me no more that they are not forgiven. After the Spirit of God has helped me, by Christ, to call God my Father, he tells me no more that the devil is my father. After he hath told me that I am not under the law, but under grace, he tells me no more that I am not under grace, but under the law, and bound over by it, for my sins, to the wrath and judgment of God; but this is the fear that the Spirit, as a spirit of bondage, worketh in the soul at first.

Quest. Can you give me further reason yet to convict me of the truth of what you say?

Answ. Yes.

1. Because as the Spirit cannot give himself the lie, so he cannot overthrow his own order of working, nor yet contradict that testimony that his servants, by his inspiration, hath given of his order of working with them. But he must do the first, if he saith to us—and that after we have received his own testimony, that we are under grace—that yet we are under sin, the law, and wrath.

And he must do the second, if—after he hath gone through the first work on us as a spirit of bondage, to the second as a spirit of adoption—he should overthrow as a spirit of bondage again what before he had built as a spirit of adoption.

And the third must therefore needs follow, that is, he overthroweth the testimony of his servants; for they have said, that now we receive the spirit of bondage again to fear no more; that is, after that we by the Holy Ghost are enabled to call God Father, Father.

2. This is evident also, because the covenant in which now the soul is interested abideth, and is everlasting, not upon the supposition of my

obedience, but upon the unchangeable purpose of God, and the efficacy of the obedience of Christ, whose blood also hath confirmed it. It is "ordered in all things, and sure," said David; and this, said he, "is all my salvation" (2 Sam 23:5). The covenant then is everlasting in itself, being established upon so good a foundation, and therefore standeth in itself everlastingly bent for the good of them that are involved in it. Hear the tenor of the covenant, and God's attesting of the truth thereof—"This is the covenant that I will make with the house of Israel, after those days, saith the Lord; I will put my laws into their mind, and write them in their hearts; and I will be to them a God, and they shall be to me a people; and they shall not teach every man his neighbour, and every man his brother, saying, Know the Lord; for all shall know me, from the least to the greatest; for I will be merciful to their unrighteousness, and their sins and their iniquities I will remember no more" (Heb 8:10-12). Now if God will do thus unto those that he hath comprised in his everlasting covenant of grace, then he will remember their sins no more, that is, unto condemnation—for so it is that he doth forget them; then cannot the Holy Ghost, who also is one with the Father and the Son, come to us again, even after we are possessed with these glorious fruits of this covenant, as a spirit of bondage, to put us in fear of damnation.

3. The Spirit of God, after it has come to me as a spirit of adoption, can come to me no more as a spirit of bondage, to put me in fear, that is, with my first fears; because, by that faith that he, even he himself, hath wrought in me, to believe and call God "Father, Father," I am united to Christ, and stand no more upon mine own legs, in mine own sins, or performances; but in his glorious righteousness before him, and before his Father; but he will not cast away a member of his body, of his flesh, and of his bones; nor will he, that the Spirit of God should come as a spirit of bondage to put him into a grounded fear of damnation, that standeth complete before God in the righteousness of Christ; for that is an apparent contradiction.

Quest. But may it not come again as a spirit of bondage, to put me into my first fears for my good?

Answ. The text saith the contrary; for we "have not received the spirit of bondage again to fear." Nor is God put to it for want of wisdom, to say and unsay, do and undo, or else he cannot do good. When we are sons, and have received the adoption of children, he doth not use to send the spirit after that to tell us we are slaves and heirs of damnation, also that we are without Christ, without the promise, without grace, and without God in the world; and yet this he must do if it comes to us after we have received him as a spirit of adoption, and put us, as a spirit of bondage, in fear as before.

[This ungodly fear wrought by the spirit of the devil.]

Quest. But by what spirit is it then that I am brought again into fears, even into the fears of damnation, and so into bondage?

Answ. By the spirit of the devil, who always labours to frustrate the faith, and hope, and comfort of the godly.

Quest. How doth that appear?

Answ. 1. By the groundlessness of such fears. 2. By the unseasonableness of them. 3. By the effects of them.

1. By the groundlessness of such fears. The ground is removed; for a grounded fear of damnation is this—I am yet in my sins, in a state of nature, under the law, without faith, and so under the wrath of God. This, I say, is the ground of the fear of damnation, the true ground to fear it; but now the man that we are talking of, is one that hath the ground of this fear taken away by the testimony and seal of the spirit of adoption. He is called, justified, and has, for the truth of this his condition, received the evidence of the spirit of adoption, and hath been thereby enabled to call God "Father, Father." Now he that hath received this, has the ground of the fear of damnation taken from him; therefore his fear, I say, being without ground, is false, and so no work of the Spirit of God.

2. By the unseasonableness of them. This spirit always comes too late. It comes after the spirit of adoption is come. Satan is always for being too soon or too late. If he would have men believe they are children, he would have them believe it while they are slaves, slaves to him and their lusts. If he would have them believe they are slaves, it is when they are sons, and have received the spirit of adoption, and the testimony, by that, of their sonship before. And this evil is rooted even in his nature—"He is a liar, and the father of it" ; and his lies are not known to saints more than in this, that he labours always to contradict the work and order of the Spirit of truth (John 8).

3. It also appears by the effects of such fears. For there is a great deal of difference betwixt the natural effects of these fears which are wrought indeed by the spirit of bondage, and those which are wrought by the spirit of the devil afterwards. The one, to wit, the fears that are wrought by the spirit of bondage, causeth us to confess the truth, to wit, that we are Christless, graceless, faithless, and so at present; that is, while he is so working in a sinful and damnable case; but the other, to wit, the spirit of the devil, when

he comes, which is after the spirit of adoption is come, he causeth us to make a lie; that is, to say we are Christless, graceless, and faithless. Now this, I say, is wholly, and in all part of it, a lie, and HE is the father of it.

Besides, the direct tendency of the fear that the Spirit of God, as a spirit of bondage, worketh in the soul, is to cause us to come repenting home to God by Jesus Christ, but these latter fears tend directly to make a man, he having first denied the work of God, as he will, if he falleth in with them, to run quite away from God, and from his grace to him in Christ, as will evidently appear if thou givest but a plain and honest answer to these questions following.

This fear driveth a man from God.

Quest. 1. Do not these fears make thee question whether there was ever a work of grace wrought in thy soul? Answ. Yes, verily, that they do. Quest. 2. Do not these fears make thee question whether ever thy first fears were wrought by the Holy Spirit of God? Answ. Yes, verily, that they do. Quest. 3. Do not these fears make thee question whether ever thou hast had, indeed, any true comfort from the Word and Spirit of God? Answ. Yes, verily, that they do. Quest. 4. Dost thou not find intermixed with these fears plain assertions that thy first comforts were either from thy fancy, or from the devil, and a fruit of his delusions? Answ. Yes, verily, that I do. Quest. 5. Do not these fears weaken thy heart in prayer? Answ. Yes, that they do. Quest. 6. Do not these fears keep thee back from laying hold of the promise of salvation by Jesus Christ? Answ. Yes; for I think if I were deceived before, if I were comforted by a spirit of delusion before, why may it not be so again? so I am afraid to take hold of the promise. Quest. 7. Do not these fears tend to the hardening of thy heart, and to the making of thee desperate? Answ. Yes, verily, that they do. Quest. 8. Do not these fears hinder thee from profiting in hearing or reading of the Word? Answ. Yes, verily, for still whatever I hear or read, I think nothing that is good belongs to me. Quest. 9. Do not these fears tend to the stirring up of blasphemies in thy heart against God? Answ. Yes, to the almost distracting of me. Quest. 10. Do not these fears make thee sometimes think, that it is in vain for thee to wait upon the Lord any longer? Answ. Yes, verily; and I have many times almost come to this conclusion, that I will read, pray, hear, company with God's people, or the like, no longer.

Well, poor Christian, I am glad that thou hast so plainly answered me; but, prithee, look back upon thy answer. How much of God dost thou think is in these things? how much of his Spirit, and the grace of his Word? Just none at all; for it cannot be that these things can be the true and natural effects of the workings of the Spirit of God: no, not as a spirit of bondage. These are not his doings. Dost thou not see the very paw of the devil in them; yea, in every one of thy ten confessions? Is there not palpably high wickedness in every one of the effects of this fear? I conclude, then, as I began, that the fear that the spirit of God, as a spirit of bondage, worketh, is good and godly, not only because of the author, but also because of the ground and effects; but yet it can last no longer as such, as producing the aforesaid conclusion, than till the Spirit, as the spirit of adoption, comes; because that then the soul is manifestly taken out of the state and condition into which it had brought itself by nature and sin, and is put into Christ, and so by him into a state of life and blessedness by grace. Therefore, if first fears come again into thy soul, after that the spirit of adoption hath been with thee, know they come not from the Spirit of God, but apparently from the spirit of the devil, for they are a lie in themselves, and their effects are sinful and devilish.

Object. But I had also such wickedness as those in my heart at my first awakening, and therefore, by your argument, neither should that be but from the devil.

Answ. So far forth as such wickedness was in thy heart, so far did the devil and thine own heart seek to drive thee to despair, and drown thee there; but thou hast forgot the question; the question is not whether then thou wast troubled with such iniquities, but whether thy fears of damnation at that time were not just and good, because grounded upon thy present condition, which was, for that thou wast out of Christ, in thy sins, and under the curse of the law; and whether now, since the spirit of adoption is come unto thee, and hath thee, and hath done that for thee as hath been mentioned; I say, whether thou oughtest for anything whatsoever to give way to the same fear, from the same ground of damnation; it is evident thou oughtest not, because the ground, the cause, is removed.

Object. But since I was sealed to the day of redemption, I have grievously sinned against God, have not I, therefore, cause to fear, as before? may not, therefore, the spirit of bondage be sent again to put me in fear, as at first? Sin was the first cause, and I have sinned now.

Answ. No, by no means; for we have not received the spirit of bondage again to fear; that is, God hath not given it us, "for God hath not given us the spirit of fear; but of power, and of love, and of a sound mind" (2 Tim 1:7). If, therefore, our first fears come upon us again, after that we have received at God's hands the spirit of love, of power, and of a sound mind, it is to be refused, though we have grievously sinned against our God. This is manifest from 1 Samuel 12:20; "Fear not; ye have done all this wickedness." That is, not with that fear which would have made them fly from God, as concluding that they were not now his people. And the reason is, because sin cannot dissolve the covenant into which the sons of God, by his grace, are taken. "If his children forsake my law, and walk not in my judgments; if they break my statutes, and keep not my commandments; then will I visit their transgressions with the rod, and their iniquity with stripes. Nevertheless, my loving-kindness will I not utterly take from him, nor suffer my faithfulness to fail" (Psa 89:30-33). Now, if sin doth not dissolve the covenant; if sin doth not cast me out of this covenant, which is made personally with the Son of God, and into the hands of which by the grace of God I am put, then ought I not, though I have sinned, to fear with my first fears.

Sin, after that the spirit of adoption is come, cannot dissolve the relation of Father and son, of Father and child. And this the church did rightly assert, and that when her heart was under great hardness, and when she had the guilt of erring from his ways, saith she. "Doubtless thou art our Father" (Isa 63:16,17). Doubtless thou art, though this be our case, and though Israel should not acknowledge us for such.

That sin dissolveth not the relation of Father and son is further evident—"When the fulness of the time was come, God sent forth his Son, made of a woman, made under the law, to redeem them that were under the law, that we might receive the adoption of sons. And because ye are sons, God hath sent forth the Spirit of his Son into your hearts, crying, [Abba, or] Father, Father." Now mark, "wherefore thou art no more a servant"; that is, no more under the law of death and damnation, "but a son; and if a son, then an heir of God through Christ" (Gal 4:4-7).

Suppose a child doth grievously transgress against and offend his father, is the relation between them therefore dissolved? Again, suppose the father should scourge and chasten the son for such offence, is the relation between them therefore dissolved? Yea, suppose the child should now, through ignorance, cry, and say, This man is now no more my father; is he, therefore, now no more his father? Doth not everybody see the folly of such arguings? Why, of the same nature is that doctrine that saith, that after we have received the spirit of adoption, that the spirit of bondage is sent to us again to put us in fear of eternal damnation.

Know then that thy sin, after thou hast received the spirit of adoption to cry unto God, Father, Father, is counted the transgression of a child, not of a slave, and that all that happeneth to thee for that transgression is but the chastisement of a father—and "what son is he whom the father chasteneth not?" It is worth your observation, that the Holy Ghost checks those who, under their chastisements for sin, forget to call God their Father—"Ye have," said Paul, "forgotten the exhortation which speaketh unto you as unto children, My son, despise not thou the chastening of the Lord, nor faint when thou art rebuked of him." Yea, observe yet further, that God's chastising of his children for their sin, is a a sign of grace and love, and not of his wrath, and thy damnation; therefore now there is no ground for the aforesaid fear—"For whom the Lord loveth he chasteneth, and scourgeth every son whom he receiveth" (Heb 12). Now, if God would not have those that have received the Spirit of the Son, however he chastises them, to forget the relation that by the adoption of sons they stand in to God, if he checks them that do forget it, when his rod is upon their backs for sin, then it is evident that those fears that thou hast under a colour of the coming again of the Spirit, as a spirit of bondage, to put thee in fear of eternal damnation, is nothing else but Satan disguised, the better to play his pranks upon thee.

I will yet give you two or three instances more, wherein it will be manifest that whatever happeneth to thee, I mean as a chastisement for sin, after the spirit of adoption is come, thou oughtest to hold fast by faith the relation of Father and son. The people spoken of by Moses are said to have lightly esteemed the rock of their salvation, which rock is Jesus Christ, and that is a grievous sin indeed, yet, saith he, "Is not God thy Father that hath bought thee?" and then puts them upon considering the days of old (Deut 32:6). They in the prophet Jeremiah had played the harlot with many lovers, and done evil things as they could; and, as another scripture hath it, gone a-whoring from under their God, yet God calls to them by the prophet, saying, "Wilt thou not from this time cry unto me, My Father, thou art the guide of my youth?" (Jer 3:4). Remember also that eminent text made mention of in 1 Samuel 12:20, "Fear not; ye have done all this wickedness" ; and labour to maintain faith in thy soul, of thy being a child, it being true that thou hast received the spirit of adoption before, and so that thou oughtest not to fall under thy first fears, because the ground is taken away, of thy eternal damnation.

Now, let not any, from what hath been said, take courage to live loose lives, under a supposition that once in Christ, and ever in Christ, and the covenant cannot be broken, nor the relation of Father and child dissolved; for they that do so, it is evident, have not known what it is to receive the spirit of adoption. It is the spirit of the devil in his own hue that suggesteth this unto them, and that prevaileth with them to do so. Shall we do evil that good may come? shall we sin that grace may abound? or shall we be base in life because God by grace hath secured us from wrath to come? God forbid; these conclusions betoken one void of the fear of God indeed, and of the spirit of adoption too. For what son is he, that because the father cannot break the relation, nor suffer sin to do it—that is, betwixt the Father and him—that will therefore say, I will live altogether after my own lusts, I will labour to be a continual grief to my Father?

[Considerations to prevent such temptations.]

Yet lest the devil (for some are "not ignorant of his devices"), should get an advantage against some of the sons, to draw them away from the filial fear of their Father, let me here, to prevent such temptations, present such with these following considerations.

First. Though God cannot, will not, dissolve the relation which the spirit of adoption hath made betwixt the Father and the Son, for any sins that such do commit, yet he can, and often doth, take away from them the comfort of their adoption, not suffering children while sinning to have the sweet and comfortable sense thereof on their hearts. He can tell how to let snares be round about them, and sudden fear trouble them. He can tell how to send darkness that they may not see, and to let abundance of waters cover them (Job 22:10,11).

Second. God can tell how to hide his face from them, and so to afflict them with that dispensation, that it shall not be in the power of all the world to comfort them. "When he hideth his face, who then can behold him?" (Job 23:8,9, 34:29).

Third. God can tell how to make thee again to possess the sins that he long since hath pardoned, and that in such wise that things shall be bitter to thy soul. "Thou writest bitter things against me," says Job, "and makest me to possess the iniquities of my youth." By this also he once made David groan and pray against it as an insupportable affliction (Job 13:26; Psa 25:7).

Fourth. God can lay thee in the dungeon in chains, and roll a stone upon thee, he can make thy feet fast in the stocks, and make thee a gazing-stock to men and angels (Lam 3:7,53,55; Job 13:27; Nahum 3:6).

Fifth. God can tell how to cause to cease the sweet operations and blessed influences of his grace in thy soul, and to make those gospel showers that formerly thou hast enjoyed to become now to thee nothing but powder and dust (Psa 51; Deut 28:24).

Sixth. God can tell how to fight against thee "with the sword of his mouth," and to make thee a butt for his arrows; and this is a dispensation most dreadful (Rev 2:16; Job 6:4; Psa 38:2-5).

Seventh. God can tell how so to bow thee down with guilt and distress that thou shalt in no wise be able to lift up thy head (Psa 40:12).

Eighth. God can tell how to break thy bones, and to make thee by reason of that to live in continual anguish of spirit: yea, he can send a fire into thy bones that shall burn, and none shall quench it (Psa 51:8; Lam 3:4, 1:13; Psa 102:3; Job 30:30).

Ninth. God can tell how to lay thee aside, and make no use of thee as to any work for him in thy generation. He can throw thee aside "as a broken vessel"

(Psa 31:12; Eze 44:10-13).

Tenth. God can tell how to kill thee, and to take thee away from the earth for thy sins (1 Cor 11:29-32).

Eleventh. God can tell how to plague thee in thy death, with great plagues, and of long continuance (Psa 78:45; Deut 28).

Twelfth. What shall I say? God can tell how to let Satan loose upon thee; when thou liest a dying he can license him then to assault thee with great temptations, he can tell how to make thee possess the guilt of all thy unkindness towards him, and that when thou, as I said, art going out of the world, he can cause that thy life shall be in continual doubt before thee, and not suffer thee to take any comfort day nor night; yea, he can drive thee even to a madness with his chastisements for thy folly, and yet all shall be done by him to thee, as a father chastiseth his son (Deut 28:65-67).

Thirteenth. Further, God can tell how to tumble thee from off thy deathbed in a cloud, he can let thee die in the dark; when thou art dying thou shalt not know whither thou art going, to wit, whether to heaven or to hell. Yea, he can tell how to let thee seem to come short of life, both in thine own eyes, and also in the eyes of them that behold thee. "Let us therefore fear," says the apostle,—though not with slavish, yet with filial fear—"lest a promise being left us of entering into his rest, any of you should seem to come short of it" (Heb 4:1).

Now all this, and much more, can God do to his as a Father by his rod and fatherly rebukes; ah, who know but those that are under them, what terrors, fears, distresses, and amazements God can bring his people into; he can put them into a furnace, a fire, and no tongue can tell what, so unsearchable and fearful are his fatherly chastisements, and yet never give them the spirit of bondage again to fear. Therefore, if thou art a son, take heed of sin, lest all these things overtake thee, and come upon thee.

Object. But I have sinned, and am under this high and mighty hand of God.

Answ. Then thou knowest what I say is true, but yet take heed of hearkening unto such temptations as would make thee believe thou art out of Christ, under the law, and in a state of damnation; and take heed also, that thou dost not conclude that the author of these fears is the Spirit of God come to thee again as a spirit of bondage, to put thee into such fears, lest unawares to thyself thou dost defy the devil, dishonour thy Father, overthrow good doctrine, and bring thyself into a double temptation.

Object. But if God deals thus with a man, how can he otherwise think but that he is a reprobate, a graceless, Christless, and faithless one?

Answ. Nay, but why dost thou tempt the Lord thy God? Why dost thou sin and provoke the eyes of his glory? Why "doth a living man complain, a man for the punishment of his sins?" (Lam 3:39). He doth not willingly afflict nor grieve the children of men; but if thou sinnest, though God should save thy soul, as he will if thou art an adopted son of God, yet he will make thee know that sin is sin, and his rod that he will chastise thee with, if need be, shall be made of scorpions; read the whole book of the Lamentations; read Job's and David's complaints; yea, read what happened to his Son, his well-beloved, and that when he did but stand in the room of sinners, being in himself altogether innocent, and then consider, O thou sinning child of God, if it is any injustice in God, yea, if it be not necessary, that thou shouldest be chastised for thy sin. But then, I say, when the hand of God is upon thee, how grievous soever it be, take heed, and beware that thou give not way to thy first fears, lest, as I said before, thou addest to thine affliction; and to help thee here, let me give you a few instances of the carriages of some of the saints under some of the most heavy afflictions that they have met with for sin.

[Carriages of some of the saints under heavy afflictions for sin.]

First. Job was in great affliction and that, as he confessed, for sin, insomuch that he said God had set him for his mark to shoot at, and that he ran upon him like a giant, that he took him by the neck and shook him to pieces, and counted him for his enemy; that he hid his face from him, and that he could not tell where to find him; yet he counted not all this as a sign of a damnable state, but as a trial, and chastisement, and said, when he was in the hottest of the battle, "when he hath tried me I shall come forth as gold." And again, when he was pressed upon by the tempter to think that God would kill him, he answers with greatest confidence, "Though he slay me, yet will I trust in him" (Job 7:20, 13:15, 14:12, 16, 19:11, 23:8-10).

Second. David complained that God had broken his bones, that he had set his face against his sins, and had taken from him the joy of his salvation: yet even at this time he saith, "O God, thou God of my salvation" (Psa 51:8,9,12,14).

Third. Heman complained that his soul was full of troubles, that God had laid him in the lowest pit, that he had put his acquaintance far from him, and was casting off his soul, and had hid his face from him. That he was afflicted from his youth up, and ready to die with trouble: he saith, moreover, that the fierce wrath of God went over him, that his terrors had cut him off; yea, that by reason of them he was distracted; and yet, even before he maketh any of these complaints, he takes fast hold of God as his, saying, "O Lord God of my salvation" (Psa 88).

Fourth. The church in the Lamentations complains that the Lord had afflicted her for her transgressions, and that in the day of his fierce anger; also that he had trodden under foot her mighty men, and that he had called the heathen against her; she says, that he had covered her with a cloud in his anger, that he was an enemy, and that he had hung a chain upon her; she adds, moreover, that he had shut out her prayer, broken her teeth with gravel stones, and covered her with ashes, and in conclusion, that he had utterly rejected her. But what doth she do under all this trial? doth she give up her faith and hope, and return to that fear that begot the first bondage? No: "The Lord is my portion, saith my soul, therefore will I hope in him" ; yea, she adds, "O Lord, thou hast pleaded the causes of my soul, thou hast redeemed my life" (Lam 1:5, 2:1,2,5, 3:7,8,16, 5:22, 3:24,31,58).

These things show, that God's people even after they have received the spirit of adoption, have fell foully into sin, and have been bitterly chastised for it; and also, that when the rod was most smart upon them, they made great conscience of giving way to their first fears wherewith they were made afraid by the Spirit as it wrought as a spirit of bondage; for indeed there is no such thing as the coming of the spirit of bondage to put us in fear the second time, as such, that is, after he is come as the spirit of adoption to the soul.

I conclude then, that that fear that is wrought by the spirit of bondage is good and godly, because the ground for it is sound; and I also conclude, that he comes to the soul as a spirit of bondage but once, and that once is before he comes as a spirit of adoption: and if therefore the same fear doth again take hold of thy heart, that is, if after thou hast received the spirit of adoption thou fearest again the damnation of thy soul, that thou art out of Christ and under the law, that fear is bad and of the devil, and ought by no means to be admitted by thee.

[How the devil worketh these fears.]

1. Quest. But since it is as you say, how doth the devil, after the spirit of adoption is come, work the child of God into those fears of being out of Christ, not forgiven, and so an heir of damnation again?

Answ. 1. By giving the lie, and by prevailing with us to give it too, to the work of grace wrought in our hearts, and to the testimony of the Holy Spirit of adoption. Or, 2. By abusing of our ignorance of the everlasting love of God to his in Christ, and the duration of the covenant of grace. Or, 3. By abusing some scripture that seems to look that way, but doth not. Or, 4. By abusing our senses and reason. Or, 5. By strengthening of our unbelief. Or, 6. By overshadowing of our judgment with horrid darkness. Or, 7. By giving of us counterfeit representations of God. Or, 8. By stirring up, and setting in a rage, our inward corruptions. Or, 9. By pouring into our hearts abundance of horrid blasphemies. Or, 10. By putting of wrong constructions on the rod, and chastising hand of God. Or, 11. By charging upon us, that our ill behaviours under the rod, and chastising hand of God, is a sign that we indeed have no grace, but are downright graceless reprobates. By these things and other like these, Satan, I say, Satan bringeth the child of God, not only to the borders, but even into the bowels of the fears of damnation, after it hath received a blessed testimony of eternal life, and that by the Holy Spirit of adoption.

[The people of God should fear his rod.]

Quest. But would you not have the people of God stand in fear of his rod, and be afraid of his judgments?

Answ. Yes, and the more they are rightly afraid of them, the less and the seldomer will they come under them; for it is want of fear that brings us into sin, and it is sin that brings us into these afflictions. But I would not have them fear with the fear of slaves; for that will add no strength against sin; but I would have them fear with the reverential fear of sons, and that is the way to depart from evil.

Quest. How is that?

Answ. Why, having before received the spirit of adoption; still to believe that he is our father, and so to fear with the fear of children, not as slaves fear a tyrant. I would therefore have them to look upon his rod, rebukes, chidings, and chastisements, and also upon the wrath wherewith he doth inflict, to be but the dispensations of their Father. This believed, maintains, or at least helps to maintain, in the heart, a son-like bowing under the rod. It also maintains in the soul a son-like confession of sin, and a justifying of God under all the rebukes that he grieveth us with. It also engageth us to come to him, to claim and lay hold of former mercies, to expect more, and to hope a good end shall be made of all God's present dispensations towards us (Micah 7:9; Lam 1:18; Psa 77:10-12; Lam 3:31-34).

Now God would have us thus fear his rod, because he is resolved to chastise us therewith, if so be we sin against him, as I have already showed; for although God's bowels turn within him, even while he is threatening his people, yet if we sin, he will lay on the rod so hard as to make us cry, "Woe unto us that we have sinned" (Lam 5:16); and therefore, as I said, we should be afraid of his judgments, yet only as afore is provided as of the rod, wrath, and judgment of a Father.

[Five considerations to move to child-like fear.]

Quest. But have you yet any other considerations to move us to fear God with child-like fear?

Answ. I will in this place give you five. 1. Consider that God thinks meet to have it so, and he is wiser in heart than thou; he knows best how to secure his people from sin, and to that end hath given them law and commandments to read, that they may learn to fear him as a Father (Job 37:24; Eccl 3:14; Deut 17:18,19). 2. Consider he is mighty in power; if he touch but with a fatherly touch, man nor angel cannot bear it; yea, Christ makes use of that argument, he "hath power to cast into hell; Fear him" (Luke 12:4,5). 3. Consider that he is everywhere; thou canst not be out of his sight or presence; nor out of the reach of his hand. "Fear ye not me? saith the Lord." "Can any hide himself in secret places that I shall not see him? saith the Lord. Do not I fill heaven and earth? saith the Lord" (Jer 5:22, 23:24). 4. Consider that he is holy, and cannot look with liking upon the sins of his own people. Therefore, says Peter, be "as obedient children, not fashioning yourselves according to the former lusts in your ignorance, but as he which hath called you is holy, so be ye holy in all manner of conversation, because it is written, Be ye holy, for I am holy. And if ye call on the Father, who without respect of persons judgeth according to every man's work, pass the time of your sojourning here in fear." 5. Consider that he is good, and has been good to thee, good in that he hath singled thee out from others, and saved thee from their death and hell, though thou perhaps wast worse in thy life than those that he left when he laid hold on thee. O this should engage thy heart to fear the Lord all the days of thy life. They "shall fear the Lord, and his goodness in the latter days" (Hosea 3:5).

And now for the present, I have done with that fear, I mean as to its first workings, to wit, to put me in fear of damnation, and shall come, in the next place, to treat

OF THE GRACE OF FEAR MORE IMMEDIATELY INTENDED IN THE TEXT.

I shall now speak to this fear, which I call a lasting godly fear; first, by way of explication; by which I shall show, FIRST. How by the Scripture it is described. SECOND. I shall show you what this fear flows from. And then, THIRD. I shall also show you what doth flow from it.

[How this Fear is described by the Scripture.]

FIRST. For the first of these, to wit, how by the Scripture this fear is described; and that, First. More generally. Second. More particularly.

First. More generally.

1. It is called a grace, that is, a sweet and blessed work of the Spirit of grace, as he is given to the elect by God. Hence the apostle says, "let us have grace, whereby we may serve God acceptably, with reverence and godly fear" (Heb 12:28). For as that fear that brings bondage is wrought in the soul by the Spirit as a spirit of bondage, so this fear, which is a fear that we have while we are in the liberty of sons, is wrought by him as he manifesteth to us our liberty; "where the Spirit of the Lord is, there is liberty," that is, where he is as a spirit of adoption, setting the soul free from that bondage under which it was held by the same Spirit while he wrought as a spirit of bondage. Hence as he is called a spirit working bondage to fear, so he, as the Spirit of the Son and of adoption, is called "the Spirit of the fear of the Lord" (Isa 11:2). Because it is that Spirit of grace that is the author, animater, and maintainer of our filial fear, or of that fear that is son-like, and that subjecteth the elect unto God, his word, and ways; unto him, his word, and ways, as a Father.

2. This fear is called also the fear of God, not as that which is ungodly is, nor yet as that may be which is wrought by the Spirit as a spirit of bondage, but by way of eminency; to wit, as a dispensation of the grace of the gospel, and as a fruit of eternal love. "I will put my fear in their hearts, that they shall not depart from me" (Jer 32:38-41).

3. This fear of God is called God's treasure, for it is one of his choice jewels, it is one of the rarities of heaven, "The fear of the Lord is his treasure" (Isa 33:6). And it may well go under such a title; for as treasure, so the fear of the Lord is not found in every corner. It is said all men have not faith, because that also is more precious than gold; the same is said about this fear—"There is no fear of God before their eyes" ; that is, the greatest part of men are

utterly destitute of this godly jewel, this treasure, the fear of the Lord. Poor vagrants, when they come straggling to a lord's house, may perhaps obtain some scraps and fragments, they may also obtain old shoes, and some sorry cast-off rags, but they get not any of his jewels, they may not touch his choicest treasure; that is kept for the children, and those that shall be his heirs. We may say the same also of this blessed grace of fear, which is called here God's treasure. It is only bestowed upon the elect, the heirs and children of the promise; all others are destitute of it, and so continue to death and judgment.

4. This grace of fear is that which maketh men excel and go beyond all men, in the account of God; it is that which beautifies a man, and prefers him above all other; "Hast thou," says God to Satan, "considered my servant Job, that there is none like him in the earth, a perfect and an upright man, one that feareth God, and escheweth evil?" (Job 1:8, 2:3). Mind it, "There is none like him, none alike him in the earth." I suppose he means either [that Job was the only most perfect and upright man] in those parts, or else he was the man that abounded in the fear of the Lord; none like him to fear the Lord, he only excelled others with respect to his reverencing of God, bowing before him, and sincerely complying with his will; and therefore is counted the excellent man. It is not the knowledge of the will of God, but our sincere complying therewith, that proveth we fear the Lord; and it is our so doing that putteth upon us the note of excelling; hereby appears our perfection, herein is manifest our uprightness. A perfect and an upright man is one that feareth God, and that because he escheweth evil. Therefore this grace of fear is that without which no part or piece of service which we do to God, can be accepted of him. It is, as I may call it, the salt of the covenant, which seasoneth the heart, and therefore must not be lacking there; it is also that which salteth, or seasoneth all our doings, and therefore must not be lacking in any of them (Lev 2:13).

5. I take this grace of fear to be that which softeneth and mollifieth the heart, and that makes it stand in awe both of the mercies and judgments of God. This is that that retaineth in the heart that due dread, and reverence of the heavenly majesty, that is meet should be both in, and kept in the heart of poor sinners. Wherefore when David described this fear, in the exercise of it, he calls it an awe of God. "Stand in awe," saith he, "and sin not" ; and again, "my heart standeth in awe of thy word" ; and again, "Let all the earth fear the Lord" ; what is that? or how is that? why? "Let all the inhabitants of the world stand in awe of him" (Psa 4:4, 119:161, 33:8). This is that therefore that is, as I said before, so excellent a thing in the eyes of God, to wit, a grace of the Spirit, the fear of God, his treasure, the salt of the covenant, that which makes men excel all others; for it is that which maketh the sinner to stand in

awe of God, which posture is the most comely thing in us, throughout all ages. But,

Second. And more particularly.

1. This grace is called "the beginning of knowledge," because by the first gracious discovery of God to the soul, this grace is begot: and again, because the first time that the soul doth apprehend God in Christ to be good unto it, this grace is animated, by which the soul is put into an holy awe of God, which causeth it with reverence and due attention to hearken to him, and tremble before him (Prov 1:7). It is also by virtue of this fear that the soul doth inquire yet more after the blessed knowledge of God. This is the more evident, because, where this fear of God is wanting, or where the discovery of God is not attended with it, the heart still abides rebellious, obstinate, and unwilling to know more, that it might comply therewith; nay, for want of it, such sinners say rather, As for God, let him "depart from us," and for the Almighty, "we desire not the knowledge of his ways."

2. This fear is called "the beginning of wisdom," because then, and not till then, a man begins to be truly spiritually wise; what wisdom is there where the fear of God is not? (Job 28:28; Psa 111:10). Therefore the fools are described thus, "For that they hated knowledge and did not choose the fear of the Lord" (Prov 1:29). The Word of God is the fountain of knowledge, into which a man will not with godly reverence look, until he is endued with the fear of the Lord. Therefore it is rightly called "the beginning of knowledge; but fools despise wisdom and instruction" (Prov 1:7). It is therefore this fear of the Lord that makes a man wise for his soul, for life, and for another world. It is this that teacheth him how he should do to escape those spiritual and eternal ruins that the fool is overtaken with, and swallowed up of for ever. A man void of this fear of God, wherever he is wise, or in whatever he excels, yet about the matters of his soul, there is none more foolish than himself; for through the want of the fear of the Lord, he leaves the best things at sixes and sevens, and only pursueth with all his heart those that will leave him in the snare when he dies.

3. This fear of the Lord is to hate evil. To hate sin and vanity. Sin and vanity, they are the sweet morsels of the fool, and such which the carnal appetite of the flesh runs after; and it is only the virtue that is in the fear of the Lord that maketh the sinner have an antipathy against it (Job 20:12). "By the fear of the Lord men depart from evil" (Prov 16:6). That is, men shun, separate themselves from, and eschew it in its appearances. Wherefore it is plain that those that love evil, are not possessed with the fear of God.

There is a generation that will pursue evil, that will take it in, nourish it, lay it up in their hearts, hide it, and plead for it, and rejoice to do it. These cannot have in them the fear of the Lord, for that is to hate it, and to make men depart from it: where the fear of God and sin is, it will be with the soul, as it was with Israel when Omri and Tibni strove to reign among them both at once, one of them must be put to death, they cannot live together (see 1 Kings 16): sin must down, for the fear of the Lord begetteth in the soul a hatred against it, an abhorrence of it, therefore sin must die, that is, as to the affections and lusts of it; for as Solomon says in another case, "where no wood is, the fire goeth out." So we may say, where there is a hatred of sin, and where men depart from it, there it loseth much of its power, waxeth feeble, and decayeth. Therefore Solomon saith again, "Fear the Lord, and depart from evil" (Prov 3:7). As who should say, Fear the Lord, and it will follow that you shall depart from evil: departing from evil is a natural consequence, a proper effect of the fear of the Lord where it is. By the fear of the Lord men depart from evil, that is, in their judgment, will, mind, and affections. Not that by the fear of the Lord sin is annihilated, or has lost its being in the soul; there still will those Canaanites be, but they are hated, loathed, abominated, fought against, prayed against, watched against, striven against, and mortified by the soul (Rom 7).

4. This fear is called a fountain of life—"The fear of the Lord is a fountain of life, to depart from the snares of death" (Prov 14:27). It is a fountain, or spring, which so continually supplieth the soul with variety of considerations of sin, of God, of death, and life eternal, as to keep the soul in continual exercise of virtue and in holy contemplation. It is a fountain of life; every operation thereof, every act and exercise thereof, hath a true and natural tendency to spiritual and eternal felicity. Wherefore the wise man saith in another place, "The fear of the Lord tendeth to life, and he that hath it shall abide satisfied; he shall not be visited with evil" (Prov 19:23). It tendeth to life; even as of nature, everything hath a tendency to that which is most natural to itself; the fire to burn, the water to wet, the stone to fall, the sun to shine, sin to defile, &c. Thus I say, the fear of the Lord tendeth to life; the nature of it is to put the soul upon fearing of God, of closing with Christ, and of walking humbly before him. "It is a fountain of life, to depart from the snares of death." What are the snares of death, but sin, the wiles of the devil, &c. From which the fear of God hath a natural tendency to deliver thee, and to keep thee in the way that tendeth to life.

5. This fear of the Lord, it is called "the instruction of wisdom" (Prov 15:33). You heard before that it is the beginning of wisdom, but here you find it called the instruction of wisdom; for indeed it is not only that which makes a man begin to be wise, but to improve, and make advantage of all those helps

and means to life, which God hath afforded to that end; that is, both to his own, and his neighbour's salvation also. It is the instruction of wisdom; it will make a man capable to use all his natural parts, all his natural wisdom to God's glory, and his own good. There lieth, even in many natural things, that, into which if we were instructed, would yield us a great deal of help to the understanding of spiritual matters; "For in wisdom has God made all the world" ; nor is there anything that God has made, whether in heaven above, or on earth beneath, but there is couched some spiritual mystery in it. The which men matter no more than they do the ground they tread on, or than the stones that are under their feet, and all because they have not this fear of the Lord; for had they that, that would teach them to think, even from that knowledge of God, that hath by the fear of him put into their hearts, that he being so great and so good, there must needs be abundance of wisdom in the things he hath made: that fear would also endeavour to find out what that wisdom is; yea, and give to the soul the instruction of it. In that it is called the instruction of wisdom, it intimates to us that its tendency is to keep all even, and in good order in the soul. When Job perceived that his friends did not deal with him in an even spirit and orderly manner, he said that they forsook "the fear of the Almighty" (Job 6:14). For this fear keeps a man even in his words and judgment of things. It may be compared to the ballast of the ship, and to the poise of the balance of the scales; it keeps all even, and also makes us steer our course right with respect to the things that pertain to God and man.

What this fear of God flows from.

SECOND. I come now to the second thing, to wit, to show you what this fear of God flows from.

First. This fear, this grace of fear, this son-like fear of God, it flows from the distinguishing love of God to his elect. "I will be their God," saith he, "and I will put my fear in their hearts." None other obtain it but those that are enclosed and bound up in that bundle. Therefore they, in the same place, are said to be those that are wrapt up in the eternal or everlasting covenant of God, and so designed to be the people that should be blessed with this fear. "I will make an everlasting covenant with them" saith God, "that I will not turn away from them to do them good, but I will put my fear in their hearts, that they shall not depart from me" (Jer 32:38-40). This covenant declares unto men that God hath, in his heart, distinguishing love for some of the children of men; for he saith he will be their God, that he will not leave them, nor yet suffer them to depart, to wit, finally, from him. Into these men's hearts he doth put his fear, this blessed grace, and this rare and effectual sign of his love, and of their eternal salvation.

Second. This fear flows from a new heart. This fear is not in men by nature; the fear of devils they may have, as also an ungodly fear of God; but this fear is not in any but where there dwelleth a new heart, another fruit and effect of this everlasting covenant, and of this distinguishing love of God. "A new heart also will I give them" ; a new heart, what a one is that? why, the same prophet saith in another place, "A heart to fear me," a circumcised one, a sanctified one (Jer 32:39; Eze 11:19, 36:26). So then, until a man receive a heart from God, a heart from heaven, a new heart, he has not this fear of God in him. New wine must not be put into old bottles, lest the one, to wit, the bottles, mar the wine, or the wine the bottles; but new wine must have new bottles, and then both shall be preserved (Matt 9:17). This fear of God must not be, cannot be found in old hearts; old hearts are not bottles out of which this fear of God proceeds, but it is from an honest and good heart, from a new one, from such an one that is also an effect of the everlasting covenant, and love of God to men.

" I will give them one heart" to fear me; there must in all actions be heart, and without heart no action is good, nor can there be faith, love, or fear, from every kind of heart. These must flow from such an one, whose nature is to produce, and bring forth such fruit. Do men gather grapes of thorns, or figs of thistles? so from a corrupt heart there cannot proceed such fruit as the fear of God, as to believe in God, and love God (Luke 6:43-45). The heart naturally is deceitful above all things, and desperately wicked; how then should there flow from such an one the fear of God? It cannot be. He, therefore, that hath not received at the hands of God a new heart, cannot fear the Lord.

Third. This fear of God flows from an impression, a sound impression, that the Word of God maketh on our souls; for without an impress of the Word, there is no fear of God. Hence it is said that God gave to Israel good laws, statutes, and judgments, that they might learn them, and in learning them, learn to fear the Lord their God. Therefore, saith God, in another place, "Gather the people together, men, and women, and children, and thy stranger that is within thy gates, that they may hear, and that they may learn and fear the Lord your God" (Deut 6:1,2, 31:12). For as a man drinketh good doctrine into his soul, so he feareth God. If he drinks it in much, he feareth him greatly; if he drinketh it in but little, he feareth him but little; if he drinketh it not in at all, he feareth him not at all. This, therefore, teacheth us how to judge who feareth the Lord; they are those that learn, and that stand in awe of the Word. Those that have by the holy Word of God the very form of itself engraven upon the face of their souls, they fear God (Rom 6:17).

But, on the contrary, those that do not love good doctrine, that give not place to the wholesome truths of the God of heaven, revealed in his Testament, to take place in their souls, but rather despise it, and the true possessors of it, they fear not God. For, as I said before, this fear of God, it flows from a sound impression that the Word of God maketh upon the soul; and therefore,

Fourth. This godly fear floweth from faith; for where the Word maketh a sound impression on the soul, by that impression is faith begotten, whence also this fear doth flow. Therefore right hearing of the Word is called "the hearing of faith" (Gal 3:2). Hence it is said again, "By faith Noah, being warned of God of things not seen as yet, moved with fear, prepared an ark to the saving of his house, by the which he condemned the world, and became heir of the righteousness which is by faith" (Heb 11:7). The Word, the warning that he had from God of things not seen as yet, wrought, through faith therein, that fear of God in his heart that made him prepare against unseen dangers, and that he might be an inheritor of unseen happiness. Where, therefore, there is not faith in the Word of God, there can be none of this fear; and where the Word doth not make sound impression on the soul, there can be none of this faith. So that as vices hang together, and have the links of a chain, dependence one upon another, even so the graces of the Spirit also are the fruits of one another, and have such dependence on each other, that the one cannot be without the other. No faith, no fear of God; devil's faith, devil's fear; saint's faith, saint's fear.

Fifth. This godly fear also floweth from sound repentance for and from sin; godly sorrow worketh repentance, and godly repentance produceth this fear— "For behold," says Paul, "this self-same thing, that ye sorrowed after a godly sort, what carefulness it wrought in you! yea, what clearing of yourselves! yea, what indignation! yea, what fear!" (2 Cor 7:10,11). Repentance is the effect of sorrow, and sorrow is the effect of smart, and smart the effect of faith. Now, therefore, fear must needs be an effect of, and flow from repentance. Sinner, do not deceive thyself; if thou art a stranger to sound repentance, which standeth in sorrow and shame before God for sin, as also in turning from it, thou hast no fear of God; I mean none of this godly fear; for that is the fruit of, and floweth from, sound repentance.

Sixth. This godly fear also flows from a sense of the love and kindness of God to the soul. Where there is no sense of hope of the kindness and mercy of God by Jesus Christ, there can be none of this fear, but rather wrath and despair, which produceth that fear that is either devilish, or else that which is only wrought in us by the Spirit, as a spirit of bondage; but these we do not discourse of now; wherefore the godly fear that now I treat of, it floweth from some sense or hope of mercy from God by Jesus Christ—"If thou,

Lord," says David, "shouldest mark iniquities, O Lord, who shall stand? But there is forgiveness with thee that thou mayest be feared" (Psa 130:3,4). "There is mercy with thee" ; this the soul hath sense of, and hope in, and therefore feareth God. Indeed nothing can lay a stronger obligation upon the heart to fear God, than sense of, or hope in mercy (Jer 33:8,9). This begetteth true tenderness of heart, true godly softness of spirit; this truly endeareth the affections to God; and in this true tenderness, softness, and endearedness of affection to God, lieth the very essence of this fear of the Lord, as is manifest by the fruit of this fear when we shall come to speak of it.

Seventh. This fear of God flows from a due consideration of the judgments of God that are to be executed in the world; yea, upon professors too. Yea further, God's people themselves, I mean as to themselves, have such a consideration of his judgments towards them, as to produce this godly fear. When God's judgments are in the earth, they effect the fear of his name, in the hearts of his own people—"My flesh trembleth for fear of thee, and I am," said David, "afraid of thy judgments" (Psa 119:120). When God smote Uzzah, David was afraid of God that day (1 Chron 13:12). Indeed, many regard not the works of the Lord, nor take notice of the operation of his hands, and such cannot fear the Lord. But others observe and regard, and wisely consider of his doings, and of the judgments that he executeth, and that makes them fear the Lord. This God himself suggesteth as a means to make us fear him. Hence he commands the false prophet to be stoned, "that all Israel might hear and fear." Hence also he commanded that the rebellious son should be stoned, "that all Israel might hear and fear." A false witness was also to have the same judgment of God executed upon him, "that all Israel might hear and fear." The man also that did ought presumptuously was to die, "that all Israel might hear and fear" (Deut 13:11, 21:21, 17:13, 19:20). There is a natural tendency in judgments, as judgments, to beget a fear of God in the heart of man, as man; but when the observation of the judgment of God is made by him that hath a principle of true grace in his soul, that observation being made, I say, by a gracious heart, produceth a fear of God in the soul of its own nature, to wit, a gracious or godly fear of God.

Eighth. This godly fear also flows from a godly remembrance of our former distresses, when we were distressed with our first fears; for though our first fears were begotten in us by the Spirit's working as a spirit of bondage, and so are not always to be entertained as such, yet even that fear leaveth in us, and upon our spirits, that sense and relish of our first awakenings and dread, as also occasioneth and produceth this godly fear. "Take heed," says God, "and keep thy soul diligently, lest thou forget the things which thine eyes have seen, and lest they depart from thy heart all the days of thy life, but teach them thy sons, and thy son's sons." But what were the things that their eyes had seen, that would so damnify them should they be forgotten? The answer is, the things which they saw at Horeb; to wit, the fire, the smoke, the darkness, the earthquake, their first awakenings by the law, by which they were brought into a bondage fear; yea, they were to remember this especially—"Specially," saith he, the day that thou stoodest before the Lord thy God in Horeb, when the Lord said unto me, Gather me the people together, and I will make them hear my words, that they may learn to fear me all the days that they shall live upon the earth" (Deut 4:9-11). The remembrance of what we saw, felt, feared, and trembled under the sense of, when our first fears were upon us, is that which will produce in our hearts this godly filial fear.

Ninth. This godly fear flows from our receiving of an answer of prayer, when we supplicated for mercy at the hand of God. See the proof for this—"If there be in the land famine, if there be pestilence, blasting, mildew, locust, or if there be caterpillar; if their enemy besiege them in the land of their cities, whatsoever plague, whatsoever sickness there be: what prayer and supplication soever be made by any man, or by all thy people Israel, which shall know every man the plague of his own heart, and spread forth his hands toward this house: then hear thou in heaven thy dwelling-place, and forgive, and do, and give to every man according to his ways, whose heart thou knowest (for thou, even thou only, knowest the hearts of all the children of men). That they may fear thee all the days of their life, that they live in the land which thou gavest unto our fathers" (1 Kings 8:37-40).

Tenth. This grace of fear also flows from a blessed conviction of the all-seeing eye of God; that is, from a belief that he certainly knoweth the heart, and seeth every one of the turnings and returnings thereof; this is intimated in the text last mentioned—"Whose heart thou knowest, that they may fear thee," to wit, so many of them as be, or shall be convinced of this. Indeed, without this conviction, this godly fear cannot be in us; the want of this conviction made the Pharisees such hypocrites—"Ye are they," said Christ, "which justify yourselves before men, but God knoweth your hearts" (Luke 16:15). The Pharisees, I say, were not aware of this; therefore they so much preferred themselves before those that by far were better than themselves, and it is for want of this conviction that men go on in such secret sins as they do, so much without fear either of God or his judgments.

Eleventh. This grace of fear also flows from a sense of the impartial judgment of God upon men according to their works. This also is manifest from the text mentioned above. And give unto every man according to his works or ways, "that they may fear thee," &c. This is also manifest by that of Peter—"And if ye call on the Father, who without respect of persons judgeth according to every man's work, pass the time of your sojourning here in fear" (1 Peter 1:17). He that hath godly conviction of this fear of God, will fear before him; by which fear their hearts are poised, and works directed with trembling, according to the will of God. Thus you see what a weighty and great grace this grace of the holy fear of God is, and how all the graces of the Holy Ghost yield mutually their help and strength to the nourishment and life of it; and also how it flows from them all, and hath a dependence upon every one of them for its due working in the heart of him that hath it. And thus much to show you from whence it flows. And now I shall come to the third thing, to wit, to show you

What flows from this godly fear.

THIRD. Having showed you what godly fear flows from, I come now, I say, to show you what proceedeth or flows from this godly fear of God, where it is seated in the heart of man. And,

First. There flows from this godly fear a godly reverence of God. "He is great," said David, "and greatly to be feared in the assembly of his saints." God, as I have already showed you, is the proper object of godly fear; it is his person and majesty that this fear always causeth the eye of the soul to be upon. "Behold," saith David, "as the eyes of servants look unto the hand of their masters, and as the eyes of a maiden unto the hand of her mistress; so our eyes wait upon the Lord our God, until that he have mercy upon us" (Psa 123:2). Nothing aweth the soul that feareth God so much as doth the glorious majesty of God. His person is above all things feared by them; "I fear God," said Joseph (Gen 42:18). That is, more than any other; I stand in awe of him, he is my dread, he is my fear, I do all mine actions as in his presence, as in his sight; I reverence his holy and glorious majesty, doing all things as with fear and trembling before him. This fear makes them have also a very great reverence of his Word; for that also, I told you, was the rule of their fear. "Princes," said David, "persecuted me without a cause, but my heart standeth in awe," in fear, "of thy word." This grace of fear, therefore, from it flows reverence of the words of God; of all laws, that man feareth the word; and no law that is not agreeing therewith (Psa 119:116). There flows from this godly fear tenderness of God's glory.

This fear, I say, will cause a man to afflict his soul, when he seeth that by professors dishonour is brought to the name of God and to his Word. Who would not fear thee, said Jeremiah, O king of nations, for to thee doth it appertain? He speaks it as being affected with that dishonour, that by the body of the Jews was continually brought to his name, his Word, and ways; he also speaks it of a hearty wish that they once would be otherwise minded.

The same saying in effect hath also John in the Revelation—"Who shall not fear thee, O Lord," said he, "and glorify thy name?" (Rev 15:4); clearly concluding that godly fear produceth a godly tenderness of God's glory in the world, for that appertaineth unto him; that is, it is due unto him, it is a debt which we owe unto him. "Give unto the Lord," said David, "the glory due unto his name." Now if there be begotten in the heart of the godly, by this grace of fear, a godly tenderness of the glory of God, then it follows of consequence, that where they that have this fear of God do see his glory diminished by the wickedness of the children of men, there they are grieved and deeply distressed. "Rivers of waters," said David, "run down mine eyes, because they keep not thy law" (Psa 119:136). Let met give you for this these following instances—

How was David provoked when Goliath defied the God of Israel (1 Sam 17:23- 29,45,46). Also, when others reproached God, he tells us that that reproach was even as "a sword in his bones" (Psa 42:10). How was Hezekiah afflicted when Rabshakeh railed upon his God (Isa 37). David also, for the love that he had to the glory of God's word, ran the hazard and reproach "of all the mighty people" (Psa 119:151, 89:50). How tender of the glory of God was Eli, Daniel, and the three children in their day. Eli died with fear and trembling of heart when he heard that "the ark of God was taken" (1 Sam 4:14-18). Daniel ran the danger of the lions' mouths, for the tender love that he had to the word and worship of God (Dan 6:10-16). The three children ran the hazard of a burning fiery furnace, rather than they would dare to dishonour the way of their God (Dan 3:13,16,20). This therefore is one of the fruits of this godly fear, to wit, a reverence of his name and tenderness of his glory.

Second. There flows from this godly fear, watchfulness. As it is said of Solomon's servants, they "watched about his bed, because of fear in the night," so it may be said of them that have this godly fear—it makes them a watchful people. It makes them watch their hearts, and take heed to keep them with all diligence, lest they should, by one or another of its flights, lead them to do that which in itself is wicked (Prov 4:23; Heb 12:15). It makes them watch, lest some temptation from hell should enter into their heart to the destroying of them (1 Peter 5:8). It makes them watch their mouths, and keep them also, at sometimes, as with a bit and bridle, that they offend not with their tongue, knowing that the tongue is apt, being an evil member, soon to catch the fire of hell, to the defiling of the whole body (James 3:2-7). It makes them watch over their ways, look well to their goings, and to make straight steps for their feet (Psa 39:1; Heb 12:13). Thus this godly fear puts the soul upon its watch, lest from the heart within, or from the devil without, or from the world, or some other temptation, something should surprise and overtake the child of God to defile him, or to cause him to defile the ways of God, and so offend the saints, open the mouths of men, and cause the enemy to speak reproachfully of religion.

Third. There flows from this fear a holy provocation to a reverential converse with saints in their religious and godly assemblies, for their further progress in the faith and way of holiness. "Then they that feared the Lord spake often one to another." Spake, that is, of God, and his holy and glorious name, kingdom, and works, for their mutual edification; "a book of remembrance was written before him for them that feared the Lord, and that thought upon his name" (Mal 3:16). The fear of the Lord in the heart provoketh to this in all its acts, not only of necessity, but of nature: it is the natural effect of this godly fear, to exercise the church in the contemplation of God, together and apart. All fear, good and bad, hath a natural propenseness in it to incline the heart to contemplate upon the object of fear, and though a man should labour to take off his thoughts from the object of his fear, whether that object was men, hell, devils, &c., yet do what he could the next time his fear had any act in it, it would return again to its object. And so it is with godly fear; that will make a man speak of, and think upon, the name of God reverentially (Psa 89:7); yea, and exercise himself in the holy thoughts of him in such sort that his soul shall be sanctified, and seasoned with such meditations. Indeed, holy thoughts of God, such as you see this fear doth exercise the heart withal, prepare the heart to, and for God. This fear therefore it is that David prayed for, for the people, when he said, "O Lord God of Abraham, Isaac, and of Israel our fathers, keep this for ever in the imagination of the thoughts of the heart of thy people, and prepare their heart unto thee" (1 Chron 29:18).

Fourth. There flows from this fear of God great reverence of his majesty, in and under the use and enjoyment of God's holy ordinances. His ordinances are his courts and palaces, his walks and places, where he giveth his presence to those that wait upon him in them, in the fear of his name. And this is the meaning of that of the apostle: "Then had the churches rest throughout all Judea, and Galilee, and Samaria, and were edified; and, walking in the fear of the Lord, and in the comfort of the Holy Ghost, were multiplied" (Acts 9:31). "And walking"—that word intendeth their use of the ordinances of God. They walked in all the commandments and ordinances of the Lord blameless. This, in Old Testament language, is called, treading God's courts, and walking in his paths. This, saith the text, they did here, in the fear of God. That is, in a great reverence of that God whose ordinances they were. "Ye shall keep my Sabbaths, and reverence my sanctuary; I am the Lord" (Lev 19:30, 26:2).

It is one thing to be conversant in God's ordinances, and another to be conversant in them with a due reverence of the majesty and name of that God whose ordinances they are: it is common for men to do the first, but none can do the last without this fear. "In thy fear," said David, "will I worship" (Psa 5:7). It is this fear of God, therefore, from whence doth flow that great reverence that his saints have in them, of his majesty, in and under the use and enjoyment of God's holy ordinances; and, consequently, that makes our service in the performance of them acceptable to God through Christ (Heb 12). For God expects that we serve him with fear and trembling, and it is odious among men, for a man in the presence, or about the service of his prince, to behave himself lightly, and without due reverence of that majesty in whose presence and about whose business he is. And if so, how can their service to God have anything like acceptation from the hand of God, that is done, not in, but without the fear of God? This service must needs be an abomination to him, and these servers must come off with rebuke.

Fifth. There flows from this godly fear of God, self-denial. That is, a holy abstaining from those things that are either unlawful or inexpedient; according to that of Nehemiah, "The former governors that had been before me, were chargeable unto the people, that had taken of them bread and wine, beside forty shekels of silver, yea, even their servants bare rule over the people: but so did not I, because of the fear of God" (Neh 5:15).

Here not was self-denial; he would not do as they did that went before him, neither himself, nor should his servants; but what was it that put him upon these acts of self-denial? The answer is, the fear of God: "but so did not I, because of the fear of God."

Now, whether by the fear of God in this place be meant his Word, or the grace of fear in his heart, may perhaps be a scruple to some, but in my judgment the text must have respect to the latter, to wit, to the grace of fear, for without that being indeed in the heart, the word will not produce that good self-denial in us, that here you find this good man to live in the daily exercise of. The fear of God, therefore, that was the cause of his self-denial, was this grace of fear in his heart. This made him to be, as was said before, tender of the honour of God, and of the salvation of his brother: yea, so tender, that rather than he would give an occasion to the weak to stumble, or be offended, he would even deny himself of that which others never sticked to do. Paul also, through the sanctifying operations of this fear of God in his heart, did deny himself even of lawful things, for the profit and commodity of his brother—"I will eat no flesh while the world standeth, lest I make my brother to offend" ; that is, if his eating of it would make his brother to offend (1 Cor 8:13).

Men that have not this fear of God in them, will not, cannot deny themselves— of love to God, and the good of the weak, who are subject to stumble at indifferent things—but where this grace of fear is, there follows self-denial; there men are tender of offending; and count that it far better becomes their profession to be of a self-denying, condescending conversation and temper, than to stand sturdily to their own liberty in things inexpedient, whoever is offended thereat. This grace of fear, therefore, is a very excellent thing, because it yieldeth such excellent fruit as this. For this self-denial, of how little esteem soever it be with some, yet the want of it, if the words of Christ be true, as they are, takes quite away from even a professor the very name of a disciple (Matt 10:37,38; Luke 14:26,27,33). They, says Nehemiah, lorded it over the brethren, but so did not I. They took bread and wine, and forty shekels of silver of them, but so did not I; yea, even their servants bare rule over the people, "but so did not I, because of the fear of God."

Sixth. There flows from this godly fear of God "singleness of heart" (Col 3:22). Singleness of heart both to God and man; singleness of heart, that is it which in another place is called sincerity and godly simplicity, and it is this, when a man doth a thing simply for the sake of him or of the law that commands it, without respect to this by-end,

or that desire of praise or of vain-glory from others; I say, when our obedience to God is done by us simply or alone for God's sake, for his Word's sake, without any regard to this or that by-end or reserve, "not with eye-service, as men-pleasers, but in singleness of heart, fearing God." A man is more subject to nothing than to swerve from singleness of heart in his service to God, and obedience to his will. How doth the Lord charge the children of Israel, and all their obedience, and that for seventy years together, with the want of singleness of heart towards him—"When ye fasted and mourned in the fifth and seventh month, even those seventy years, did ye at all fast unto me, even to me? And when ye did eat, and when ye did drink, did not ye eat for yourselves, and drink for yourselves?" (Zech 7:5,6).

They wanted this singleness of heart in their fasting, and in their eating, in their mourning, and in their drinking; they had double hearts in what they did. They did not as the apostle bids; "whether ye eat or drink, or whatsoever ye do, do all to the glory of God." And the reason of their want of this thing was, they wanted this fear of God; for that, as the apostle here saith, effecteth singleness of heart to God, and makes a man, as John said of Gaius, "do faithfully whatsoever he doth" (3 John 5). And the reason is, as hath been already urged, for that grace of fear of God retaineth and keepeth upon the heart a reverent and awful sense of the dread majesty and all-seeing eye of

God, also a due consideration of the day of account before him; it likewise maketh his service sweet and pleasing, and fortifies the soul against all discouragements; by this means, I say, the soul, in its service to God or man, is not so soon captivated as where there is not this fear, but through and by it its service is accepted, being single, sincere, simple, and faithful; when others, with what they do, are cast into hell for their hypocrisy, for they mix not what they do with godly fear. Singleness of heart in the service of God is of such absolute necessity, that without it, as I have hinted, nothing can be accepted; because where that is wanting, there wanteth love to God, and to that which is true holiness indeed. It was this singleness of heart that made Nathanael so honourable in the eyes of Jesus Christ. "Behold," said he, "an Israelite indeed, in whom there is no guile" (John 1:47). And it was the want of it that made him so much abhor the Pharisees. They wanted sincerity, simplicity, and godly sincerity in their souls, and so became an abhorrence in his esteem. Now, I say, this golden grace, singleness of heart, it flows from this godly fear of God.

Seventh. There flows from this godly fear of God, compassion and bowels to those of the saints that are in necessity and distress. This is manifest in good Obadiah; it is said of him, "That he took an hundred" of the Lord's "prophets, and hid them by fifty in a cave, and fed them with bread and water," in the days when Jezebel, that tyrant, sought their lives to destroy them (1 Kings 18:3,4). But what was it that moved so upon his heart, as to cause him to do this thing? Why, it was this blessed grace of the fear of God. "Now Obadiah," saith the text, "feared the Lord greatly, for it was so, when Jezebel cut off the prophets of the Lord, that Obadiah took an hundred prophets, and hid them by fifty in a cave, and fed them with bread and water." This was charity to the distressed, even to the distressed for the Lord's sake.

Had not Obadiah served the Lord, yea, had he not greatly feared him, he would not have been able to do this thing, especially as the case then stood with him, and also with the church at that time, for then Jezebel sought to slay all that indeed feared the Lord; yea, and the persecution prevailed so much at that time, that even Elijah himself thought that she had killed all but him. But now, even now, the fear of God in this good man's heart put forth itself into acts of mercy though attended with so imminent danger. See here, therefore, that the fear of God will put forth itself in the heart where God hath put it, even to show kindness, and to have compassion upon the distressed servants of God, even under Jezebel's nose; for Obadiah dwelt in Ahab's house, and Jezebel was Ahab's wife, and a horrible persecutor, as was said before: yet Obadiah will show mercy to the poor because he feared God, yea, he will venture her displeasure, his place, and neck, and all, but he will be merciful to his brethren in distress. Cornelius, also, being a man possessed with this fear of God, became a very free-hearted and open-handed man to the poor—"He feared God, and gave much alms to the people." Indeed this fear, this godly fear of God, it is a universal grace; it will stir up the soul unto all good duties. It is a fruitful grace; from it, where it is, floweth abundance of excellent virtues; nor without it can there be anything good, or done well, that is done. But,

Eighth. There flows from this fear of God hearty, fervent, and constant prayer. This also is seen in Cornelius, that devout man. He feared God; and what then? why, he gave much alms to the people, "and prayed to God alway" (Acts 10:1,2).

Did I say that hearty, fervent, and constant prayer flowed from this fear of God? I will add, that if the whole duty, and the continuation of it, be not managed with this fear of God, it profiteth nothing at all. It is said of our Lord Jesus Christ himself, "He was heard in that he feared." He prayed, then, because he feared, because he feared God, and therefore was his prayer accepted of him, even because he feared—"He was heard in that he feared" (Heb 5:7). This godly fear is so essential to right prayer, and right prayer is such an inseparable effect and fruit of this fear, that you must have both or none; he that prayeth not feareth not God, yea, he that prayeth not fervently and frequently feareth him not; and so he that feareth him not cannot pray; for if prayer be the effect of this fear of God, then without this fear, prayer, fervent prayer, ceaseth. How can they pray or make conscience of the duty that fear not God? O prayerless man, thou fearest not God! Thou wouldest not live so like a swine or a dog in the world as thou dost, if thou fearest the Lord.

Ninth. There floweth from this fear of God a readiness or willingness, at God's call, to give up our best enjoyments to his disposal. This is evident in Abraham, who at God's call, without delay, rose early in the morning to offer up his only and well-beloved Isaac a burnt-offering in the place where God should appoint him. It was a rare thing that Abraham did; and had he not had this rare grace, this fear of God, he would not, he could not have done to God's liking so wonderful a thing. It is true the Holy Ghost also makes this service of Abraham to be the fruit of his faith—"By faith Abraham offered up Isaac, and he that had received the promises offered up his only-begotten son" (Heb 11; James 2). Aye, and without doubt love unto God, in Abraham, was not wanting in this his service, nor was this grace of fear; nay, in the story where it is recorded. There it is chiefly accounted for the fruit of his godly fear, and that by an angel from heaven—"And the angel called out of heaven, and said, Abraham, Abraham. And he said, Here am I. And he said, Lay not thine hand upon the lad, neither do thou anything unto him, for now

I know that thou fearest God, seeing thou hast not withheld thy son, thine only son, from me" (Gen 22:11,12). Now I know it; now, now thou hast offered up thine only Isaac, thine all, at the bidding of thy God. Now I know it. The fear of God is not presently discerned in the heart and life of a man. Abraham had long before this done many a holy duty, and showed much willingness of heart to observe and do the will of God; yet you find not, as I remember, that he had this testimony from heaven that he feared God till now; but now he has it, now he has it from heaven. "Now I know that thou fearest God." Many duties may be done—though I do not say that Abraham did them— without the fear of God; but when a man shall not stick at, or withhold, his darling from God, when called upon by God to offer it up unto him, that declareth, yea, and gives conviction to angels, that now he feareth God.

Tenth. There floweth from this godly fear humility of mind. This is evident, because, when the apostle cautions the Romans against the venom of spiritual pride, he directs them to the exercise of this blessed grace of fear as its antidote. "Be not high-minded," saith he, "but fear" (Rom 11:20). Pride, spiritual pride, which is here set forth by the word "high-minded," is a sin of a very high and damnable nature; it was the sin of the fallen angels, and is that which causeth men to fall into the same condemnation—"Lest being lifted up with pride, he fall into the condemnation of the devil." Pride, I say, it damns a professor with the damnation of devils, with the damnation of hell, and therefore it is a deadly, deadly sin. Now against this deadly sin is set the grace of humility; that comely garment, for so the apostle calls it, saying, "be clothed with humility." But the question is now, how we should attain to, and live in, the exercise of this blessed and comely grace? to which the apostle answers, Fear; be afraid with godly fear, and thence will flow humility—"Be not high-minded, but fear." That is, Fear, or be continually afraid and jealous of yourselves, and of your own naughty hearts, also fear lest at some time or other the devil, your adversary, should have advantage of you.

Fear, lest by forgetting what you are by nature, you also forget the need that you have of continual pardon, support, and supplies from the Spirit of grace, and so grow proud of your own abilities, or of what you have received of God, and fall into the condemnation of the devil. Fear, and that will make you little in your own eyes, keep you humble, put you upon crying to God for protection, and upon lying at his foot for mercy; that will also make you have low thoughts of your own parts, your own doings, and cause you to prefer your brother before yourself, and so you will walk in humiliation, and be continually under the teachings of God, and under his conduct in your way. The humble, God will teach—"The meek will he guide in judgment, the meek will he teach his way." From this grace of fear then flows this excellent and comely thing, humility; yea, it also is maintained by this fear. Fear takes off a man from trusting to himself, it puts a man upon trying of all things, it puts a man upon desiring counsel and help from heaven, it makes a man ready and willing to hear instruction, and makes a man walk lowly, softly, and so securely in the way.

Eleventh. There flows from this grace of fear, hope in the mercy of God—"The Lord taketh pleasure in them that fear him, in them that hope in his mercy" (Psa 147:11). The latter part of the text is an explanation of the former: as if the psalmist had said, They be the men that fear the Lord, even they that hope in his mercy; for true fear produceth hope in God's mercy. And it is further manifest thus. Fear, true fear of God inclineth the heart to a serious inquiry after that way of salvation which God himself hath prescribed; now the way that God hath appointed, by the which the sinner is to obtain the salvation of his soul, is his mercy as so and so set forth in the Word, and godly fear hath special regard to the Word. To this way, therefore, the sinner with this godly fear submits his soul, rolls himself upon it, and so is delivered from that death into which others, for want of this fear of God, do headlong fall.

It is, as I also hinted before, the nature of godly fear to be very much putting the soul upon the inquiry which is, and which is not, the thing approved of God, and accordingly to embrace it or shun it. Now I say, this fear having put the soul upon a strict and serious inquiry after the way of salvation, at last it finds it to be by the mercy of God in Christ; therefore this fear putteth the soul upon hoping also in him for eternal life and blessedness; by which hope he doth not only secure his soul, but becomes a portion of God's delight—"The Lord takes pleasure in them that fear him, in them that hope in his mercy."

Besides, this godly fear carrieth in it self-evidence that the state of the sinner is happy, because possessed with this happy grace. Therefore, as John saith, "We know we have passed from death unto life, because we love the brethren" (1 John 3:14). So here, "The Lord taketh pleasure in them that fear him, in them that hope in his mercy." If I fear God, and if my fearing of him is a thing in which he taketh such pleasure, then may I boldly venture to roll myself for eternal life into the bosom of his mercy, which is Christ. This fear also produceth hope; if therefore, poor sinner, thou knowest thyself to be one that is possessed with this fear of God, suffer thyself to be persuaded therefore to hope in the mercy of God for salvation, for the Lord takes pleasure in thee. And it delights him to see thee hope in his mercy.

Twelfth. There floweth from this godly fear of God an honest and conscientious use of all those means which God hath ordained, that we should be conversant in for our attaining salvation. Faith and hope in God's mercy is that which secureth our justification and hope, and as you have heard, they do flow from this fear. But now, besides faith and hope, there is a course of life in those things in which God hath ordained us to have our conversation, without which there is no eternal life. "Ye have your fruit unto holiness, and the end everlasting life" ; and again, "without holiness no man shall see the Lord." Not that faith and hope are deficient, if they be right, but they are both of them counterfeit when not attended with a reverent use of all the means: upon the reverent use of which the soul is put by this grace of fear. "Wherefore, beloved," said Paul, "as ye have always obeyed, not as in my presence only, but now much more in mine absence, work out your own salvation with fear and trembling" (Rom 6:22; Heb 12:14; Phil 2:11).

There is a faith and hope of mercy that may deceive a man (though the faith of God's elect, and the hope that purifies the heart never will), because they are alone, and not attended with those companions that accompany salvation (Heb 6:3-8). But now this godly fear carries in its bowels, not only a moving of the soul to faith and hope in God's mercy, but an earnest provocation to the holy and reverent use of all the means that God has ordained for a man to have his conversation in, in order to his eternal salvation. "Work out your salvation with fear." Not that work is meritorious, or such that can purchase eternal life, for eternal life is obtained by hope in God's mercy; but this hope, if it be right, is attended with this godly fear, which fear putteth the soul upon a diligent use of all those means that may tend to the strengthening of hope, and so to the making of us holy in all manner of conversation, that we may be meet to be partakers of the inheritance of the saints in light. For hope purifieth the heart, if fear of God shall be its companion, and so maketh a man a vessel of mercy prepared unto glory. Paul bids Timothy to fly pride, covetousness, doting about questions, and the like, and to "follow after righteousness, godliness, faith, love, patience; to fight the good fight of faith, and to lay hold on eternal life" (1 Tim 6).

So Peter bids that we "add to our faith virtue; and to virtue knowledge; and to knowledge temperance; and to temperance patience; and to patience godliness; and to godliness brotherly kindness; and to brotherly kindness charity" ; adding, "for if these things be in you and abound, they make you that ye shall neither be barren nor unfruitful in the knowledge of our Lord Jesus Christ. Wherefore the rather, brethren, give diligence to make your calling and election sure; for if ye do these things, ye shall never fall. For so an entrance shall be ministered unto you abundantly into the everlasting kingdom of our Lord and Saviour Jesus Christ" (2 Peter 1:5-11). The sum of all which is that which was mentioned before; to wit, "to work out our own salvation with fear and trembling." For none of these things can be conscientiously done, but by and with the help of this blessed grace of fear.

Thirteenth. There flows from this fear, this godly fear, a great delight in the holy commands of God, that is, a delight to be conformable unto them. "Blessed is the man that feareth the Lord, that delighteth greatly in his commandments" (Psa 112:1). This confirmeth that which was said before, to wit, that this fear provoketh to a holy and reverent use of the means; for that cannot be, when there is not an holy, yea, a great delight in the commandments. Wherefore this fear maketh the sinner to abhor that which is sin, because that is contrary to the object of his delight. A man cannot delight himself at the same time in things directly opposite one to another, as sin and the holy commandment is; therefore Christ saith of the servant, he cannot love God and mammon—"Ye cannot serve God and mammon." If he cleaves to the one, he must hate and despise the other; there cannot at the same time be service to both, because that themselves are at enmity one with the other. So is sin and the commandment. Therefore if a man delighteth himself in the commandment, he hateth that which is opposite, which is sin: how much more when he greatly delighteth in the commandment? Now, this holy fear of God it taketh the heart and affections from sin, and setteth them upon the holy commandment. Therefore such a man is rightly esteemed blessed. For no profession makes a man blessed but that which is accompanied with an alienation of the heart from sin, nor doth anything do that when this holy fear is wanting. It is from this fear then, that love to, and delight in, the holy commandment floweth, and so by that the sinner is kept from those falls and dangers of miscarrying that other professors are so subject to: he greatly delights in the commandment.

Fourteenth. Lastly, There floweth from this fear of God, enlargement of heart. "Then thou shalt see, and flow together, and thine heart shall fear, and be enlarged" (Isa 60:5). "Thine heart shall fear, and be enlarged," enlarged to God-ward, enlarged to his ways, enlarged to his holy people, enlarged in love after the salvation of others. Indeed when this fear of God is wanting, though the profession be never so famous, the heart is shut up and straitened, and nothing is done in that princely free spirit which is called "the spirit of the fear of the Lord" (Psa 51:12; Isa 11:2). But with grudging, legally, or with desire of vain-glory, this enlargedness of heart is wanting, for that flows from this fear of the Lord.

Thus have I showed you both what this fear of God is, what it flows from, and also what doth flow from it. I come now to show you some

OF THE PRIVILEGES OF THEM THAT THUS DO FEAR THE LORD.

Having thus briefly handled in particular thus far this fear of God, I shall now show you certain of the excellent privileges of them that fear the Lord, not that they are not privileges that have been already mentioned; for what greater privileges than to have this fear producing in the soul such excellent things so necessary for us for good, both with reference to this world, and that which is to come? But because those fourteen above named do rather flow from this grace of fear where it is, than from a promise to the person that hath it, therefore I have chosen rather to discourse of them as the fruits and effects of fear, than otherwise. Now, besides all these, there is entailed by promise to the man that hath this fear many other blessed privileges, the which I shall now in a brief way lay open unto you.

First Privilege, then. That man that feareth the Lord, has a grant and a license "to trust in the Lord," with an affirmation that he is their help, and their shield— "Ye that fear the Lord, trust in the Lord; he is their help and their shield" (Psa 115:11). Now what a privilege is this! an exhortation in general to sinners, as sinners, to trust in him, is a privilege great and glorious; but for a man to be singled out from his neighbours, for a man to be spoken to from heaven, as it were by name, and to be told that God hath given him a license, a special and peculiar grant to trust in him, this is abundantly more; and yet this is the grant that God hath given that man! He hath, I say, a license to do it—a license indicted by the Holy Ghost, and left upon record for those to be born that shall fear the Lord, to trust in him. And not only so, but as the text affirmeth, "he is their help and their shield." Their help under all their weaknesses and infirmities, and a shield to defend them against all the assaults of the devil and this world. So then, the man that feareth the Lord is licensed to make the Lord his stay and God of his salvation, the succour and deliverer of his soul. He will defend him because his fear is in his heart. O ye servants of the Lord, ye that fear him, live in the comfort of this; boldly make use of it when you are in straits, and put your trust under the shadow of his wings, for indeed he would have you do so, because you do fear the Lord.

Second Privilege. God hath also proclaimed concerning the man that feareth the Lord, that he will also be his teacher and guide in the way that he shall choose, and hath moreover promised concerning such, that their soul shall dwell at ease—"What man is he that feareth the Lord?" says David, "him shall he teach in the way that he shall choose" (Psa 25:12). Now, to be taught of God, what like it? yea, what like to be taught in the way that thou shalt choose? Thou hast chosen the way to life, God's way; but perhaps thy ignorance about it is so great, and those that tempt thee to turn aside so many and so subtle, that they seem to outwit thee and confound thee with their guile. Well, but the Lord whom thou fearest will not leave thee to thy ignorance, nor yet to thine enemies' power or subtlety, but will take it upon himself to be thy teacher and thy guide, and that in the way that thou hast chosen. Hear, then, and behold thy privilege, O thou that fearest the Lord; and whoever wanders, turns aside, and swerveth from the way of salvation, whoever is benighted, and lost in the midst of darkness, thou shalt find the way to the heaven and the glory that thou hast chosen.

Further, He doth not only say, that he will teach them the way, for that must of necessity be supplied, but he says also that he will teach such in it—"Him shall he teach in the way that he shall choose." This argueth that, as thou shalt know, so the way shall be made, by the communion that thou shalt have with God therein, sweet and pleasant to thee. For this text promiseth unto the man that feareth the Lord, the presence, company, and discovery of the mind of God, while he is going in the way that he hath chosen. It is said of the good scribe, that he is instructed unto, as well as into, the way of the kingdom of God (Matt 13:52). Instructed unto; that is, he hath the heart and mind of God still discovered to him in the way that he hath chosen, even all the way from this world to that which is to come, even until he shall come to the very gate and door of heaven. What the disciples said was the effect of the presence of Christ, to wit, "that their hearts did burn within them while he talked to them by the way," shall be also fulfilled in thee, he will meet with thee in the way, talk with thee in the way; he will teach thee in the way that thou shalt choose (Luke 24:32).

Third Privilege. Dost thou fear the Lord? he will open his secret unto thee, even that which he hath hid and keeps close from all the world, to wit, the secret of his covenant and of thy concern therein—"The secret of the Lord is with them that fear him, and he will shew them his covenant" (Psa 25:14). This, then, further confirmeth what was said but just above; his secret shall be with them, and his covenant shall be showed unto them. His secret, to wit, that which hath been kept hid from ages and generations; that which he manifesteth only to the saints, or holy ones; that is, his Christ, for he it is that is hid in God, and that no man can know but he to whom the Father shall reveal him (Matt 11:27).

But O! what is there wrapped up in this Christ, this secret of God? why, all treasures of life, of heaven, and happiness—"In him are hid all the treasures of wisdom and knowledge." And "in him dwelleth all the fulness of the Godhead bodily" (Col 2).

This also is that hidden One, that is so full of grace to save sinners, and so full of truth and faithfulness to keep promise and covenant with them, that their eyes must needs convey, even by every glance they make upon his person, offices, and relation, such affecting ravishments to the heart, that it would please them that see him, even to be killed with that sight. This secret of the Lord shall be, nay is, with them that fear him, for he dwelleth in their heart by faith. "And he will shew them his covenant." That is, the covenant that is confirmed of God in Christ, that everlasting and eternal covenant, and show him too that he himself is wrapped up therein, as in a bundle of life with the Lord his God. These are the thoughts, purposes, and promises of God to them that fear him.

Fourth Privilege. Dost thou fear the Lord? his eye is always over thee for good, to keep thee from all evil—"Behold the eye of the Lord is upon them that fear him, upon them that hope in his mercy; to deliver their soul from death, and to keep them alive in famine" (Psa 33:18,19). His eye is upon them; that is, to watch over them for good. He that keepeth Israel neither slumbers nor sleeps. His eyes are upon them, and he will keep them as a shepherd doth his sheep; that is, from those wolves that seek to devour them, and to swallow them up in death. His eyes are upon them; for they are the object of his delight, the rarities of the world, in whom, saith he, is all my delight. His eye is upon them, as I said before, to teach and instruct them—"I will instruct thee and teach thee in the way which thou shalt go; I will guide thee with mine eye" (Psa 32:8; 2 Chron 7:15,16). The eye of the Lord, therefore, is upon them, not to take advantage of them, to destroy them for their sins, but to guide, to help, and deliver them from death; from that death that would feed upon their souls—"To deliver their soul from death and to keep them alive in famine." Take death here for death spiritual, and death eternal; and the famine here, not for that that is for want of bread and water, but for that which comes on many for want of the Word of the Lord (Rev 20:14; Amos 8:11,12); and then the sense is this, the man that feareth the Lord shall neither die spiritually nor eternally; for God will keep him with his eye from all those things that would in such a manner kill him. Again, should there be a famine of the Word; should there want both the Word and them that preach it in the place that thou dost dwell, yet bread shall be given thee, and thy water shall be sure; thou shalt not die of the famine, because thou fearest God. I say, that man shall not, behold he shall not, because he feareth God, and this the next head doth yet more fully manifest.

Fifth Privilege. Dost thou fear God? fear him for this advantage more and more—"O fear the Lord, ye his saints, for there is no want to them that fear him. The young lions do lack and suffer hunger, but they that seek the Lord," that fear him, "shall not want any good thing" (Psa 34:9,10). Not anything that God sees good for them shall those men want that fear the Lord. If health will do them good, if sickness will do them good, if riches will do them good, if poverty will do them good, if life will do them good, if death will do them good, then they shall not want them, neither shall any of these come nigh them, if they will not do them good. The lions, the wicked people of the world that fear not God, are not made sharers in this great privilege; all things fall out to them contrary, because they fear not God. In the midst of their sufficiency, they are in want of that good that God puts into the worst things that the man that feareth God doth meet with in the world.

Sixth Privilege. Dost thou fear God? he hath given charge to the armies of heaven to look after, take charge of, to camp about, and to deliver thee—"The angel of the Lord encampeth round about them that fear him, and delivereth them" (Psa 34:7). This also is a privilege entailed to them that in all generations fear the Lord. The angels, the heavenly creatures, have it in commission to take the charge of them that fear the Lord; one of them is able to slay of men in one night 185,000. These are they that camped about Elisha like horses of fire, and chariots of fire, when the enemy came to destroy him.

They also helped Hezekiah against the band of the enemy, because he feared God (2 Kings 6:17; Isa 37:36; Jer 26:19). "The angel of the Lord encampeth round about them" ; that is, lest the enemy should set upon them on any side; but let him come where he will, behind or before, on this side or that, the angel of the Lord is there to defend them. "The angel." It may be spoken in the singular number, perhaps, to show that every one that feareth God hath his angel to attend on him, and serve him. When the church, in the Acts, was told that Peter stood at the door and knocked; at first they counted the messenger mad, but when she did constantly affirm it, they said, It is his angel (Acts 12:13-15). So Christ saith of the children that came unto him, "their angels behold the face of my Father which is in heaven." Their angels; that is, those of them that feared God, had each of them his angel, who had a charge from God to keep them in their way. We little think of this, yet this is the privilege of them that fear the Lord; yea, if need be, they shall all come down to help them and to deliver them, rather than, contrary to the mind of their God, they should by any be abused—"Are they not all ministering spirits, sent forth to minister for them who shall be heirs of salvation?" (Heb 1:14).

[Quest.] But how do they deliver them? for so says the text—"The angel of the Lord encampeth round about them that fear him, and delivereth them." Answ. The way that they take to deliver them that fear the Lord, is sometimes by smiting of their enemies with blindness, that they may not find them; and so they served the enemies of Lot (Gen 19:10,11). Sometimes by smiting of them with deadly fear; and so they served those that laid siege against Samaria (2 Kings 7:6). And sometimes by smiting of them even with death itself; and thus they served Herod, after he had attempted to kill the apostle James, and also sought to vex certain others of the church (Acts 12). These angels that are servants to them that fear the Lord, are them that will, if God doth bid them, revenge the quarrel of his servants upon the stoutest monarch on earth. This, therefore, is a glorious privilege of the men that fear the Lord. Alas! they are, some of them, so mean that they are counted not worth taking notice of by the high ones of the world; but their betters do respect them. The angels of God count not themselves too good to attend on them, and camp about them to deliver them. This, then, is the man that hath his angel to wait upon him, even he that feareth God.

Seventh Privilege. Dost thou fear the Lord? salvation is nigh unto thee— "Surely his salvation is nigh them that fear him, that glory may dwell in our land" (Psa 85:9). This is another privilege for them that fear the Lord. I told you before, that the angel of the Lord did encamp about them, but now he saith, "his salvation is also nigh them"; the which although it doth not altogether exclude the conduct of angels, but include them; yet it looketh further. "Surely his salvation," his saving, pardoning grace, "is nigh them that fear him"; that is, to save them out of the hand of their spiritual enemies. The devil, and sin, and death, do always wait even to devour them that fear the Lord, but to deliver them from these his salvation doth attend them. So then, if Satan tempts, here is their salvation nigh; if sin, by breaking forth, beguiles them, here is God's salvation nigh them; yea, if death itself shall suddenly seize upon them, why, here is their God's salvation nigh them.

I have seen that great men's little children must go no whither without their nurses be at hand. If they go abroad, their nurses must go with them; if they go to meals, their nurses must go with them; if they go to bed, their nurses must go with them; yea, and if they fall asleep, their nurses must stand by them. O my brethren, those little ones that fear the Lord, they are the children of the highest, therefore they shall not walk alone, be at their spiritual meats alone, go to their sick-beds, or to their graves alone; the salvation of their God is nigh them, to deliver them from the evil. This is then the glory that dwells in the land of them that fear the Lord.

Eighth Privilege. Dost thou fear the Lord? hearken yet again—"The mercy of the Lord is from everlasting to everlasting upon them that fear him, and his righteousness unto children's children" (Psa 103:17). This still confirms what was last asserted, that is, that his salvation is nigh unto them. His salvation, that is, pardoning mercy, that is nigh them. But mind it, there he says it is nigh them; but here it is upon them. His mercy is upon them, it covereth them all over, it encompasseth them about as with a shield. Therefore they are said in another place to be clothed with salvation, and covered with the robe of righteousness. The mercy of the Lord is upon them, that is, as I said, to shelter and defend them. The mercy, the pardoning preserving mercy, the mercy of the Lord is upon them, who is he then that can condemn them? (Rom 8).

But there yet is more behind, "The mercy of the Lord is from everlasting to everlasting upon them." It was designed for them before the world was, and shall be upon them when the world itself is ended; from everlasting to everlasting it is on them that fear him. This from everlasting to everlasting is that by which, in another place, the eternity of God himself is declared—"From everlasting to everlasting, thou art God" (Psa 90:2). The meaning, then, may be this; that so long as God hath his being, so long shall the man that feareth him find mercy at his hand. According to that of Moses—"The eternal God is thy refuge, and underneath are the everlasting arms; and he shall thrust out the enemy from before thee, and shall say, Destroy them" (Deut 33:27).

Child of God, thou that fearest God, here is mercy nigh thee, mercy enough, everlasting mercy upon thee. This is long-lived mercy. It will live longer than thy sin, it will live longer than temptation, it will live longer than thy sorrows, it will live longer than thy persecutors. It is mercy from everlasting to contrive thy salvation, and mercy to everlasting to weather it out with all thy adversaries. Now what can hell and death do to him that hath this mercy of God upon him? And this hath the man that feareth the Lord. Take that other blessed word, and O thou man that fearest the Lord, hang it like a chain of gold about thy neck—"As the heaven is high above the earth, so great is his mercy toward them that fear him" (Psa 103:11). If mercy as big, as high, and as good as heaven itself will be a privilege, the man that feareth God shall have a privilege.

Ninth Privilege. Dost thou fear God?—"Like as a father pitieth his children, so the Lord pitieth them that fear him" (Psa 103:13).

" The Lord pitieth them that fear him" ; that is, condoleth and is affected, feeleth and sympathizeth with them in all their afflictions. It is a great matter for a poor man to be in this manner in the affections of the great and mighty, but for a poor sinner to be thus in the heart and affections of God, and they that fear him are so, this is astonishing to consider. "In his love and in his pity he redeemed them." In his love and in his pity! "In all their affliction he was afflicted, and the angel of his presence saved them; in his love and in his pity he redeemed them, and he bare them, and carried them all the days of old" (Isa 63:9). I say, in that he is said to pity them, it is as much as to say, he condoleth, feeleth, and sympathizeth with them in all their afflictions and temptations. So that this is the happiness of him that feareth God, he has a God to pity him and to be touched with all his miseries. It is said in Judges, "His soul was grieved for the misery of Israel" (Judg 10:16). And in the Hebrews, he is "touched with the feeling of our infirmities," and can "succour them that are tempted" (4:15, 2:17,18).

But further, let us take notice of the comparison. "As a father pitieth his children, so the Lord pitieth them that fear him." Here is not only pity, but the pity of a relation, a father. It is said in another place; "Can a woman," a mother, "forget her sucking child, that she should not have compassion on the son of her womb? yea, they may, yet will not I forget thee." The pity of neighbours and acquaintance helpeth in times of distress, but the pity of a father and a mother is pity with an over and above. "The Lord," says James, "is very pitiful, and of tender mercy." Pharaoh called Joseph his tender father, because he provided for him against the famine, but how tender a father is God! how full of bowels! how full of pity! (James 5:11; Gen 41:43). It is said, that when Ephraim was afflicted, God's bowels were troubled for him, and turned within him towards him. O that the man that feareth the Lord did but believe the pity and bowels that are in the heart of God and his father towards him (Jer 31:18-20).

Tenth Privilege. Dost thou fear God?—"He will fulfil the desire of them that fear him; he also will hear their cry, and will save them" (Psa 145:19). Almost all those places that make mention of the men that fear God, do insinuate as if they still were under affliction, or in danger by reason of an enemy. But I say, here is still their privilege, their God is their father and pities them—"He will fulfil the desire of them that fear him." Where now is the man that feareth the Lord? let him hearken to this. What sayest thou, poor soul? will this content thee, the Lord will fulfil thy desires? It is intimated of Adonijah, that David his father did let him have his head and his will in all things. "His father," says the text, "had not displeased him at any time in (so much as) saying, Why hast thou done so?" (1 Kings 1:6). But here is more, here is a promise to grant thee the whole desire of thy heart, according to the prayer of holy David, "The Lord grant thee, according to thine own heart, and fulfil all thy counsel." And again, "The Lord fulfil all thy petitions" (Psa 20).

O thou that fearest the Lord, what is thy desire? All my desire, says David, is all my salvation (2 Sam 23:5), so sayest thou, "All my salvation" is "all my desire." Well, the desire of thy soul is granted thee, yea, God himself hath engaged himself even to fulfil this thy desire—"He will fulfil the desire of them that fear him, he also will hear their cry, and will save them." O this desire when it cometh, what a tree of life will it be to thee! Thou desirest to be rid of thy present trouble; the Lord shall rid thee out of trouble. Thou desirest to be delivered from temptation; the Lord shall deliver thee out of temptation. Thou desirest to be delivered from thy body of death; and the Lord shall change this thy vile body, that it may be like to his glorious body. Thou desirest to be in the presence of God, and among the angels in heaven. This thy desire also shall be fulfilled, and thou shalt be made equal to the angels (Exo 6:6; 2 Peter 2:9; Phil 3:20,21; Luke 16:22, 20:35,36). O but it is long first! Well, learn first to live upon thy portion in the promise of it, and that will make thy expectation of it sweet. God will fulfil thy desires, God will do it, though it tarry long. Wait for it, because it will surely come, it will not tarry.

Eleventh Privilege. Dost thou fear God?—"The Lord taketh pleasure in them that fear him" (Psa 147:11). They that fear God are among his chief delights. He delights in his Son, he delights in his works, and takes pleasure in them that fear him. As a man takes pleasure in his wife, in his children, in his gold, in his jewels; so the man that fears the Lord is the object of his delight. He takes pleasure in their prosperity, and therefore sendeth them health from the sanctuary, and makes them drink of the river of his pleasures (Psa 35:27). "They shall be abundantly satisfied with the fatness of thy house; and thou shalt make them drink of the river of thy pleasures" (Psa 36:8). That or those that we take pleasure in, that or those we love to beautify and adorn with many ornaments. We count no cost too much to be bestowed on those in whom we place our delight, and whom we make the object of our pleasure. And even thus it is with God. "For the Lord taketh pleasure in his people," and what follows? "he will beautify the meek with salvation" (Psa 149:4).

Those in whom we delight, we take pleasure in their actions; yea, we teach them, and give them such rules and laws to walk by, as may yet make them that we love more pleasurable in our eyes. Therefore they that fear God, since they are the object of his pleasure, are taught to know how to please him in everything (1 Thess 4:1). And hence it is said, that he is ravished with their looks, that he delighteth in their cry, and that he is pleased with their walking (Can 4:9; Prov 15:8, 11:20).

Those in whom we delight and take pleasure, many things we will bear and put up that they do, though they be not according to our minds. A man will suffer that in, and put up that at, the hand of the child or wife of his pleasure, that he will not pass by nor put up in another. They are my jewels, says God, even them that fear me; and I will spare them, in all their comings-short of my will, "even as a man spareth his own son that serveth him" (Mal 3:16,17).

O how happy is the man that feareth God! His good thoughts, his good attempts to serve him, and his good life pleases him, because he feareth God.

You know how pleasing in our eyes the actions of our children are, when we know that they do what they do even of a reverent fear and awe of us; yea, though that which they do amounts but to little, we take it well at their hands, and are pleased therewith. The woman that cast in her two mites into the treasury, cast in not much, for they both did but make one farthing; yet how doth the Lord Jesus trumpet her up, he had pleasure in her, and in her action (Mark 12:41-44). This, therefore, that the Lord taketh pleasure in them that fear him, is another of their great privileges.

Twelfth Privilege. Dost thou fear God? the least dram of that fear giveth the privilege to be blessed with the biggest saint—"He will bless them that fear the Lord, small and great" (Psa 115:13). This word small may be taken three ways—1. For those that are small in esteem, for those that are but little accounted of (Judg 6:15; 1 Sam 18:23). Art thou small or little in this sense, yet if thou fearest God, thou art sure to be blessed. "He will bless them that fear him, small and great," be thou never so small in the world's eyes, in thine own eyes, in the saints' eyes, as sometimes one saint is little in another saint's eye; yet thou, because thou fearest God, art put among the blessed. 2. By small, sometimes is meant those that are but small of stature, or young in years, little children, that are easily passed by and looked over: as those that sang Hosanna in the temple were, when the Pharisees deridingly said of them to Christ, "Hearest thou what these say?" (Matt 21:16). Well, but Christ would not despise them, of them that feared God, but preferred them by the Scripture testimony far before those that did contemn them. Little children, how small soever, and although of never so small esteem with men, shall also, if they fear the Lord, be blessed with the greatest saints—"He will bless them that fear him, small and great." 3. By small may sometimes be meant those that are small in grace or gifts; these are said to be the least in the church, that is, under this consideration, and so are by it least esteemed (Matt 25:45). Thus also is that of Christ to be understood, "Inasmuch as ye did it not to one of the least of these, ye did it not to me" (1 Cor 6:4).

Art thou in thine own thoughts, or in the thoughts of others, of these last small ones, small in grace, small in gifts, small in esteem upon this account, yet if thou fearest God, if thou fearest God indeed, thou art certainly blessed with the best of saints. The least star stands as fixed, as the biggest of them all, in heaven. "He will bless them that fear him, small and great." He will bless them, that is, with the same blessing of eternal life. For the different degrees of grace in saints doth not make the blessing, as to its nature, differ. It is the same heaven, the same life, the same glory, and the same eternity of felicity that they are in the text promised to be blessed with. That is observable which I mentioned before, where Christ at the day of judgment particularly mentioneth and owneth the least—"Inasmuch as ye did it not to one of the least." The least then was there, in his kingdom and in his glory, as well as the biggest of all. "He will bless them that fear him, small and great." The small are named first in the text, and are so the first in rank; it may be to show that though they may be slighted and little set by in the world, yet they are much set by in the eyes of the Lord.

Are great saints only to have the kingdom, and the glory everlasting? Are great works only to be rewarded? works that are done by virtue of great grace, and the abundance of the gifts of the Holy Ghost? No: "Whosoever shall give to drink unto one of these little ones a cup of cold water only, in the name of a disciple, verily I say unto you, he shall in no wise lose his (a disciple's) reward." Mark, here is but a little gift, a cup of cold water, and that given to a little saint, but both taken special notice of by our Lord Jesus Christ (Matt 10:42). "He will give reward to his servants the prophets, and to his saints, and to them that fear his name, small and great" (Rev 11:18). The small, therefore, among them that fear God, are blessed with the great, as the great, with the same salvation, the same glory, and the same eternal life; and they shall have, even as the great ones also shall, as much as they can carry; as much as their hearts, souls, bodies, and capacities can hold.

Thirteenth Privilege. Dost thou fear God? why, the Holy Ghost hath on purpose indited for thee a whole psalm to sing concerning thyself. So that thou mayest even as thou art in thy calling, bed, journey, or whenever, sing out thine own blessed and happy condition to thine own comfort and the comfort of thy fellows. The psalm is called the 128th Psalm; I will set it before thee, both as it is in the reading and in the singing Psalms—

" Blessed is every one that feareth the Lord, that walketh in his ways. For thou shalt eat the labour of thine hands: happy shalt thou be, and it shall be well with thee. Thy wife shall be as a fruitful vine by the sides of thine house; thy children, like olive plants round about thy table. Behold, that thus shall the man be blessed that feareth the Lord. The Lord shall bless thee out of Zion; and thou shalt see the good of Jerusalem all the days of thy life. Yea, thou shalt see thy children's children, and peace upon Israel."

AS IT IS SUNG.
Blessed art thou that fearest God,
And walkest in his way:
For of thy labour thou shalt eat;
Happy art thou, I say!

Like fruitful vines on thy house side,
So doth thy wife spring out;
Thy children stand like olive plants
Thy table round about.

Thus art thou blest that fearest God,
And he shall let thee see
The promised Jerusalem,
And her felicity.
Thou shalt thy children's children see,
To thy great joy's increase;
And likewise grace on Israel,
Prosperity and peace.

And now I have done with the privileges when I have removed one objection.

Object. But the Scripture says, "perfect love casteth our fear" ; and therefore it seems that saints, after that a spirit of adoption is come, should not fear, but do their duty, as another Scripture saith, without it (1 John 4:18; Luke 1:74,75).

Answ. Fear, as I have showed you, may be taken several ways. 1. It may be taken for the fear of devils. 2. It may be taken for the fear of reprobates. 3. It may be taken for the fear that is wrought in the godly by the Spirit as a spirit of bondage; or, 4. It may be taken for the fear that I have been but now discoursing of.

Now the fear that perfect love casts out cannot be that son-like, gracious fear of God, that I have in this last place been treating of; because that fear that love casts out hath torment, but so has not the son-like fear. Therefore the fear that love casts out is either that fear that is like the fear of devils and reprobates, or that fear that is begot in the heart by the Spirit of God as a spirit of bondage, or both; for, indeed, all these kinds of fear have torment, and therefore may be cast out; and are so by the spirit of adoption, which is called the spirit of faith and love, when he comes with power into the soul; so that without this fear we should serve him. But to argue from these texts that we ought not to fear God, or to mix fear with our worship of him, is as much as to say that by the spirit of adoption we are made very rogues; for not to fear God is by the Scripture applied to such (Luke 23:40). But for what I have affirmed the Scripture doth plentifully confirm, saying, "Happy is the man that feareth alway." And again, "It shall be well with them that fear God, which fear before him." Fear, therefore; the spirit of the fear of the

Lord is a grace that greatly beautifies a Christian, his words, and all his ways: "Wherefore now let the fear of the Lord be upon you; take heed, and do it, for there is no iniquity with the Lord our God, nor respect of persons, nor taking of gifts" (2 Chron 19:7).

I come now to make some use and application of this doctrine.

THE USE OF THIS DOCTRINE.

Having proceeded thus far about this doctrine of the fear of God, I now come to make some use and application of the whole; and my

[USE FIRST, of Examination.]

FIRST USE shall be a USE OF EXAMINATION. Is this fear of God such an excellent thing? Is it attended with so many blessed privileges? Then this should put us, every soul of us, upon a diligent examination of ourselves, to wit, whether this grace be in us or not, for if it be, then thou art one of these blessed ones to whom belong these glorious privileges, for thou hast an interest in every of them; but if it shall appear that this grace is not in thee, then thy state is fearfully miserable, as hath partly been manifest already, and will further be seen in what comes after. Now, the better to help thee to consider, and not to miss in finding out what thou art in thy self-examination, I will speak to this— First. In general. Second. In particular.

First. In general. No man brings this grace into the world with him. Every one by nature is destitute of it; for naturally none fear God, there is no fear of God, none of this grace of fear before their eyes, they do not so much as know what it is; for this fear flows, as was showed before, from a new heart, faith, repentance and the like; of which new heart, faith, and repentance, if thou be void, thou art also void of this godly fear. Men must have a mighty change of heart and life, or else they are strangers to this fear of God. Alas, how ignorant are the most of this! Yea, and some are not afraid to say they are not changed, nor desire so to be. Can these fear God? can these be possessed with this grace of fear? No: "Because they have no changes, therefore they fear not God" (Psa 55:19; Psa 36:1; Rom 3:18).

Wherefore, sinner, consider whoever thou art that art destitute of this fear of God, thou art void of all other graces; for this fear, as also I have showed, floweth from the whole stock of grace where it is. There is not one of the graces of the Spirit, but this fear is in the bowels of it; yea, as I may say, this fear is the flower and beauty of every grace; neither is there anything, let it look as much like grace as it will, that will be counted so indeed, if the fruit thereof be not this fear of God; wherefore, I say again, consider well of this matter, for as thou shalt be found with reference to this grace, so shall thy judgment be. I have but briefly treated of this grace, yet have endeavoured, with words as fit as I could, to display it in its colours before thy face, first by showing you what this fear of God is, then what it flows from, as also what doth flow from it; to which, as was said before, I have added several privileges that are annexed to this fear, that by all, if it may be, thou mayest see it if thou hast it, and thyself without it if thou hast it not. Wherefore I refer thee thither again for information in this thing; or if thou art loath to give the book a second reading, but wilt go on to the end now thou art gotten hither; then

Second and particularly, I conclude with these several propositions concerning those that fear not God.

1. That man that is proud, and of a high and lofty mind, fears not God. This is plain from the exhortation, "Be not high-minded, but fear" (Rom 11:20). Here you see that a high mind and the fear of God are set in direct opposition the one to the other; and there is in them, closely concluded by the apostle, that where indeed the one is, there cannot be the other; where there is a high mind, there is not the fear of God; and where there is the fear of God, the mind is not high but lowly. Can a man at the same time be a proud man, and fear God too? Why, then, is it said God beholdeth every one that is proud, and abases him? and again, He beholds the proud afar off? He therefore that is proud of his person, of his riches, of his office, of his parts, and the like, feareth not God. It is also manifest further, for God resisteth the proud, which he would not do, if he feared him, but in that he sets him at such a distance from him, in that he testifies that he will abase him and resist him, it is evident that he is not the man that hath this grace of fear; for that man, as I have showed you, is the man of God's delight, the object of his pleasure (Psa 138:6; James 4:6; 1 Peter 5:5; Mal 4:1).

2. The covetous man feareth not God. This also is plain from the Word, because it setteth covetousness and the fear of God in direct opposition. Men that fear God are said to hate covetousness (Exo 18:21). Besides, the covetous man is called an idolater, and is said to have no part in the kingdom of Christ and of God. And again, "The wicked boasteth of his heart's desire, and blesseth the covetous, whom the Lord abhorreth" (Eze 33:31; Eph 5:5; Psa 10:3). Hearken to this, you that hunt the world to take it, you that care not how you get, so you get the world. Also you that make even religion your stalking-horse to get the world, you fear not God. And what will you do whose hearts go after your covetousness? you who are led by covetousness up and down, as it were by the nose; sometimes to swear, to lie, to cozen, and cheat and defraud, when you can get the advantage to do it. You are far, very far, from the fear of God. "Ye adulterers and adulteresses," for so the covetous are called, "know ye not that the friendship of the world is enmity with God? whosoever, therefore, will be a friend of the world, is the enemy of God" (James 4:4).

3. The riotous eaters of flesh have not the fear of God. For this is done "without fear" (Jude 12). Gluttony is a sin little taken notice of, and as little repented of by those that use it, but yet it is odious in the sight of God, and the practice of it a demonstration of the want of his fear in the heart: yea, so odious is it, that God forbids that his people should so much as company with such. "Be not," saith he, "among wine-bibbers, among riotous eaters of flesh" (Prov 23:20). And he further tells us, that they that are such, are spots and blemishes to those that keep them company, for indeed they fear not God (2 Peter 2:13; Rom 13:13; 1 Peter 4:4). Alas! some men are as if they were for nought else born but to eat and to drink, and pamper their carcasses with the dainties of this world, quite forgetting why God sent them hither; but such, as is said, fear not God, and so consequently are of the number of them upon whom the day of judgment will come at unawares (Luke 21:34).

4. The liar is one that fears not God. This also is evident from the plain text, "Thou hast lied," saith the Lord, "and hast not remembered me, nor laid it to thy heart: have not I held my peace even of old," saith the Lord, "and thou fearest me not?" (Isa 57:11). What lie this was is not material; it was a lie, or a course of lying that is here rebuked, and the person or persons in this practice, as is said, were such as feared not God; a course of lying and the fear of God cannot stand together. This sin of lying is a common sin, and it walketh in the world in several guises. There is the profane scoffing liar, there is the cunning artificial liar, there is the hypocritical religious liar, with liars of other ranks and degrees. But none of them all have the fear of God, nor shall any of them, they not repenting, escape the damnation of hell—"All liars shall have their part in the lake which burneth with fire and brimstone" (Rev 21:8). Heaven and the New Jerusalem are not a place for such—"And there shall in no wise enter into it anything that defileth, neither whatsoever worketh abomination, or maketh a lie" (v 27). Therefore another scripture says that all liars are without—"For without are dogs, and sorcerers, and whoremongers, and murderers, and idolaters, and whosoever loveth and maketh a lie" (Rev 22:15). But this should not be their sentence, judgment, and condemnation, if they that are liars were such as had in them this blessed fear of God.

5. They fear not God who cry unto him for help in the time of their calamity, and when they are delivered, they return to their former rebellion. This, Moses, in a spirit of prophecy, asserteth at the time of the mighty judgment of the hail. Pharaoh then desired him to pray to God that he would take away that judgment from him. Well, so I will, said Moses, "But as for thee and thy servants, I know that ye will not yet fear the Lord God" (Exo 9:30). As who should say, I know that so soon as this judgment is removed, you will to your old rebellion again. And what greater demonstration can be given that such a

man feareth not God, than to cry to God to be delivered from affliction to prosperity, and to spend that prosperity in rebellion against him? This is crying for mercies that they may be spent, or that we may have something to spend upon our lusts, and in the service of Satan (John 4:1-3). Of these God complains in the sixteenth of Ezekiel, and in the second of Hosea—"Thou hast," saith God, "taken thy fair jewels of my gold and of my silver, which I had given thee, and madest to thyself images" &c. (Eze 16:17). This was for want of the fear of God. Many of this kind there be now in the world, both of men, and women, and children; art not thou that readest this book of this number? Hast thou not cried for health when sick, for wealth when poor, when lame for strength, when in prison for liberty, and then spent all that thou gottest by thy prayer in the service of Satan, and to gratify thy lusts? Look to it, sinner, these things are signs that with thy heart thou fearest not God.

6. They fear not God that way-lay his people and seek to overthrow them, or to turn them besides the right path, as they are journeying from hence to their eternal rest. This is evident from the plain text, "Remember," saith God, "what Amalek did unto thee by the way when ye were come forth out of Egypt; how he met thee by the way, and smote the hindmost of thee, even all that were feeble behind thee, when thou wast faint and weary, and he feared not God" (Deut 25:17,18). Many such Amalekites there be now in the world that set themselves against the feeble of the flock, against the feeble of the flock especially, still smiting them, some by power, some with the tongue, some in their lives and estates, some in their names and reputations, by scandals, slanders, and reproach, but the reason of this their ungodly practice is this, they fear not God. For did they fear him, they would be afraid to so much as think, much more of attempting to afflict and destroy, and calumniate the children of God; but such there have been, such there are, and such there will be in the world, for all men fear not God.

7. They fear not God who see his hand upon backsliders for their sins, and yet themselves will be backsliders also. "I saw," saith God, "when for all the causes whereby backsliding Israel committed adultery, I had put her away, and given her a bill of divorce, yet her treacherous sister Judah feared not, but went and played the harlot also" (Jer 3:8, 2:19). Judah saw that her sister was put away, and delivered by God into the hands of Shalmaneser, who carried her away beyond Babylon, and yet, though she saw it, she went and played the harlot also—a sign of great hardness of heart, and of the want of the fear of God indeed. For this fear, had it been in her heart, it would have taught her to have trembled at the judgment that was executed upon her sister, and not to have gone and played the harlot also: and not to have done it while her sister's judgment was in sight and memory. But what is it that a

heart that is destitute of the fear of God will not do? No sin comes amiss to such: yea, they will sin, they will do that themselves, for the doing of which they believe some are in hell-fire, and all because they fear not God.

But pray observe, if those that take not warning when they see the hand of God upon backsliders, are said to have none of the fear of God, have they it, think you, that lay stumbling-blocks in the way of God's people, and use devices to cause them to backslide, yea, rejoice when they can do this mischief to any? and yet many of this sort there are in the world, that even rejoice when they see a professor fall into sin, and go back from his profession, as if they had found some excellent thing.

8. They fear not God who can look upon a land as wallowing in sin, and yet are not humbled at the sight thereof. "Have ye," said God by the prophet to the Jews, "forgotten the wickedness of your fathers, and the wickedness of the kings of Judah, and the wickedness of their wives, which they have committed in the land of Judah and in the streets of Jerusalem? They are not humbled to this day, neither have they feared, nor walked in my law" (Jer 44:9,10). Here is a land full of wickedness, and none to bewail it, for they wanted the fear of God, and love to walk in his law. But how say you, if they that are not humbled at their own and others' wickedness are said not to fear, or have the fear of God, what shall we think or say of such that receive, that nourish and rejoice in such wickedness? Do they fear God? Yea, what shall we say of such that are the inventors and promoters of wickedness, as of oaths, beastly talk, or the like? Do they, do you think, fear God? Once again, what shall we say of such that cannot be content to be wicked themselves, and to invent and rejoice in other men's wickedness, but must hate, reproach, vilify and abuse those that they cannot persuade to be wicked? Do they fear God?

9. They that take more heed to their own dreams than to the Word of God, fear not God. This also is plain from the Word—"For in the multitude of dreams, there are also divers vanities, but fear thou God" ; that is, take heed unto his Word (Eccl 5:7; Isa 8:20). Here the fearing of God is opposed to our overmuch heeding dreams: and there is implied, that it is for want of the fear of God that men so much heed those things. What will they say to this that give more heed to a suggestion that ariseth from their foolish hearts, or that is cast in thither by the devil, than they do to the holy Word of God? These are "filthy dreamers." Also, what shall we say to those that are more confident of the mercy of God to their soul, because he hath blessed them with outward things, than they are afraid of his wrath and condemnation, though the whole of the Word of God doth fully verify the same? These are "filthy dreamers" indeed.

A dream is either real, or so by way of semblance, and so some men dream sleeping, and some waking (Isa 29:7). And as those that a man dreams sleeping are caused either by God, Satan, business, flesh, or the like; so are they that a man dreams waking, to pass by those that we have in our sleep. Men, when bodily awake, may have dreams, that is, visions from heaven; such are all they that have a tendency to discover to the sinner his state, or the state of the church according to the Word. But those that are from Satan, business, and the flesh, are such—especially the first and last, to wit, from Satan and the flesh—as tend to embolden men to hope for good in a way disagreeing with the Word of God.

These Jude calls "filthy dreamers," such whose principles were their dreams, and they led them "to defile the flesh," that is, by fornication and uncleanness; "to despise dominion," that the reins might be laid upon the neck of their lusts; "to speak evil of dignities," of those that God had set over them, for their governing in all the law and testament of Christ, these dreamt that to live like brutes, to be greedy of gain, and to take away for it, as Cain and Balaam did by their wiles, the lives of the owners thereof, would go for good coin in the best of trials. These also Peter speaks of (2 Peter 2). And he makes their dreams, that Jude calls so, their principle and errors in life and doctrine; you may read of them in that whole chapter, where they are called cursed children, and so by consequence such as fear not God.

10. They fear not God, who are sorcerers, adulterers, false swearers, and that oppress the hireling of his wages. It is a custom with some men to keep back by fraud from the hireling that which by covenant they agreed to pay for their labour; pinching, I say, and paring from them their due that of right belongs to them, to the making of them cry in "the ears of the Lord of sabaoth" (James 5:4). These fear not God; they are reckoned among the worst of men, and in their day of account God himself will bear witness against them. "And I," saith God, "will come near to you to judgment; and I will be a swift witness against the adulterers, and against the false swearers, and against those that oppress the hireling in his wages, the widow and the fatherless, and that turn aside the stranger from his right, and fear not me, saith the Lord" (Mal 3:5).

11. They fear not God, who instead of pitying of, rail at God's people in their affliction, temptations, and persecutions, and rather rejoice and skip for joy, than sympathize with them in their sorrow. Thus did David's enemies, thus did Israel's enemies, and thus did the thief, he railed at Christ when he hanged upon the cross, and was for that, even by his fellow, accounted for one that feared not God (Luke 23:40; Psa 35:1,22-26. Read Oba 10-15; Jer

48:2-6). This is a common thing among the children of men, even to rejoice at the hurt of them that fear God, and it ariseth even of an inward hatred to godliness. They hate you, saith Christ, because they hated me. Therefore Christ takes what is done to his, in this, as done unto himself, and so to holiness of life. But this falls hard upon such as despise at, and rejoice to see, God's people in their griefs, and that take the advantage, as dogged Shimei did, to augment the griefs and afflictions of God's people (2 Sam 16:5-8). These fear not God, they do this of enmity, and their sin is such as will hardly be blotted out (1 Kings 2:8,9).

12. They fear not God, who are strangers to the effects of fear. "If I be a master, where is my fear?" That is, show that I am so by your fear of me in the effects of your fear of me. "You offer polluted bread upon mine altar." This is not a sign that you fear me, ye offer the blind for sacrifices, where is my fear? ye offer the lame and the sick, these are not the effects of the fear of God (Mal 1:6-8). Sinner, it is one thing to say, I fear God, and another to fear him indeed. Therefore, as James says, show me thy faith by thy works, so here God calls for a testimony of thy fear by the effects of fear. I have already showed you several effects of fear; if thou art a stranger to them, thou art a stranger to this grace of fear. Therefore, to conclude this, it is not a feigned profession that will do; nothing is good here, but what is salted with this fear of God, and they that fear him are men of truth, men of singleness of heart, perfect, upright, humble, holy men; wherefore, reader, examine, and again, I say examine, and lay the Word and thy heart together, before that thou concludest that thou fearest God.

What! fear God, and in a state of nature? fear God without a change of heart and life? What! fear God and be proud, and covetous, a wine-bibber, and a riotous eater of flesh? How! fear God and a liar, and one that cries for mercies to spend them upon thy lusts? This would be strange. True, thou mayest fear as devils do, but what will that profit? Thou mayest by thy fear be driven away from God, from his worship, people, and ways, but what will that avail? It may be thou mayest so fear at present, as to be a little stopped in thy sinful course; perhaps thou hast got a knock from the Word of God, and are at present a little dazzled and hindered from being in thy former and full career after sin; but what of that? if by the fear that thou hast, thy heart is not united to God, and to the love of his Son, Word, and people, thy fear is nothing worth. Many men also are forced to fear God, as underlings are forced to fear those that are by force above them. If thou only thus fearest God, it is but a false fear; it flows not from love to God: this fear brings not willing subjection, which indeed brings the effect of right fear; but being over-mastered like an hypocrite, thou subjected thyself by feigned obedience, being forced, I say, by mere dread to do it (Psa 66:3).

It is said of David, "that the fame of him went out into all lands, and the Lord brought the fear of him upon all nations" (1 Chron 14:17). But what, did they now love David? did they now choose him to be their king? no verily; they, many of them, rather hated him, and, when they could, made resistance against him. They did even as thou dost—feared, but did not love; feared, but did not choose his government that ruled over them. It is also said of Jehoshaphat, when God had subdued before him Ammon, Moab, and mount Seir, that "the fear of God was on all the kingdoms of these countries, when they had heard that the Lord fought against the enemies of Israel" (2 Chron 20:29). But, I say, was this fear, that is called now the fear of God, anything else, but a dread of the greatness of power of the king? No verily, nor did that dread bring them into a willing subjection to, and liking of his laws and government; it only made them like slaves and underlings, stand in fear of his executing the vengeance of God upon them.

Therefore still, notwithstanding this fear, they were rebels to him in their hearts, and when occasion and advantage offered themselves, they showed it by rising in rebellion against Israel. This fear therefore provoked but feigned and forced obedience, a right emblem of the obedience of such, who being still enemies in their minds to God, are forced by virtue of present conviction to yield a little, even of fear to God, to his Word, and to his ordinances. Reader, whoever thou art, think of this, it is thy concern, therefore do it, and examine, and examine again, and look diligently to thy heart in thine examination, that it beguile thee not about this thy so great concern, as indeed the fear of God is.

One thing more, before I leave thee, let me warn thee of. Take heed of deferring to fear the Lord. Some men, when they have had conviction upon their heart that the fear of God is not in them, have through the overpowering of their corruptions yet deferred and put off the fear of God from them, as it is said of them in Jeremiah: "This people hath a revolting and a rebellious heart; they are revolted and gone. Neither say they in their heart, Let us now fear the Lord" (Jer 5:23,24). They saw that the judgments of God attended them because they did not yet fear God, but that conviction would not prevail with them to say, "Let us now fear the Lord." They were for deferring to fear him still; they were for putting off his fear from them longer. Sinner, hast thou deferred to fear the Lord? is thy heart still so stubborn as not to say yet, "Let us fear the Lord?" O! the Lord hath taken notice of this thy rebellion, and is preparing some dreadful judgment for thee. "Shall I not visit for these things? saith the Lord; shall not my soul be avenged on such a nation as this?" (v 29). Sinner, why shouldest thou pull vengeance down upon thee? why shouldest thou pull vengeance down from heaven upon thee? Look up, perhaps thou hast already been pulling this great while, to pull it down upon thee. O! pull no longer; why shouldest thou be thine own executioner? Fall down upon thy knees, man, and up with thy heart and thy hands to the God that dwells in the heavens; cry, yea cry aloud, Lord, unite mine heart to fear thy name, and do not harden mine heart from thy fear. Thus holy men have cried before thee, and by crying have prevented judgment.

[A few things that may provoke thee to fear the Lord.]

Before I leave this use, let me give thee a few things, that, if God will, may provoke thee to fear the Lord.

1. The man that feareth not God, carrieth it worse towards him than the beast, the brute beast, doth carry it towards that man. "The fear of you, and the dread of you, shall be upon every beast of the earth," yea, "and upon every fowl of the air," and "upon all that moveth upon the earth, and upon all the fishes of the sea" (Gen 9:2).

Mark, all my creatures shall fear you, and dread you, says God. None of them shall be so hardy as to cast of all reverence of you. But what a shame is this to man, that God should subject all his creatures to him, and he should refuse to stoop his heart to God? The beast, the bird, the fish, and all, have a fear and dread of man, yea, God has put it in their hearts to fear man, and yet man is void of fear and dread, I mean of godly fear of him, that thus lovingly hath put all things under him. Sinner, art thou not ashamed, that a silly cow, a sheep, yea, a swine, should better observe the law of his creation, than thou dost the law of thy God?

2. Consider, he that will not fear God, God will make him fear him whether he will or no. That is, he that doth not, will not now so fear him, as willingly to bow before him, and put his neck into his yoke. God will make him fear him when he comes to take vengeance on him. Then he will surround him with terror, and with fear on every side, fear within, and fear without; fear shall be in the way, even in the way that thou goest when thou art going out of this world; and that will be dreadful fear (Eccl 12:5). "I will bring their fears upon them," saith the Lord (Isa 66:4).

3. He that fears not God now, the Lord shall laugh at his fears then. Sinner, God will be even with all them that choose not to have his fear in their hearts: for as he calls and they hear not now, so they shall cry, yea, howl then, and he will laugh at their fears. "I will laugh," saith he, "at their destruction; I will mock when their fear cometh, when your fear cometh as desolation and your destruction cometh as a whirlwind, when distress and

anguish cometh upon you; then shall they call upon me, but I will not answer: they shall seek me early, but they shall not find me, for that they hated knowledge, and did not choose the fear of the Lord" (Prov 1:27-29).

Sinner! thou thinkest to escape the fear; but what wilt thou do with the pit? Thou thinkest to escape the pit; but what wilt thou do with the snare? The snare, say you, what is that? I answer, it is even the work of thine own hands. "The wicked is snared in the work of his own hands," he is "snared by the transgression of his lips" (Psa 9:16; Prov 12:13).

Sinner! what wilt thou do when thou comest into this snare; that is, into the guilt and terror that thy sins will snaffle thee with, when they, like a cord, are fastened about thy soul? This snare will bring thee back again to the pit, which is hell, and then how wilt thou do to be rid of thy fear? The fear, pit, and the snare shall come upon thee, because thou fearest not God.

Sinner! art thou one of them that hast cast off fear? poor man, what wilt thou do when these three things beset thee? whither wilt thou fly for help? And where wilt thou leave thy glory? If thou fliest from the fear, there is the pit; if thou fliest from the pit, there is the snare.

[USE SECOND, an exhortation to fear God.]

SECOND USE. My next word shall be AN EXHORTATION TO FEAR GOD. I mean an exhortation to saints—"O fear the Lord, ye his saints, for there is no want to them that fear him." Not but that every saint doth fear God, but as the apostle saith in another case, "I beseech you, do it more and more." The fear of the Lord, as I have showed you, is a grace of the new covenant, as other saving graces are, and so is capable of being stronger or weaker, as other graces are. Wherefore I beseech you, fear him more and more.

It is said of Obadiah, that he feared the Lord greatly: every saint fears the Lord, but every saint does not greatly fear him. O there are but few Obadiahs in the world, I mean among the saints on earth: see the whole relation of him (1 Kings 18). As Paul said of Timothy, "I have none like-minded," so it may be said of some concerning the fear of the Lord; they have scarce a fellow. So it was with Job, "There is none like him in the earth, one that feareth God," &c. (Job 1:8). There was even none in Job's day that feared God like him, no, there was not one like him in all the earth, but doubtless there were more in the world that feared God; but this fearing of him greatly, that is the thing that saints should do, and that was the thing that Job did do, and in that he did outstrip his fellows. It is also said of Hananiah, that "he was a faithful man, and feared God above many" (Neh 7:2). He also had got, as to the exercise of, and growth in, this grace, the start of many of his brethren. He "feared God above many." Now then, seeing this grace admits of degrees, and is in some stronger, and in some weaker, let us be all awakened as to other graces, so to this grace also. That like as you abound in everything, in faith, in utterance, in knowledge, and in all diligence, and in your love to us, see that ye abound in this grace also. I will labour to enforce this exhortation upon you by several motives.

First. Let God's distinguishing love to you be a motive to you to fear him greatly. He hath put his fear in thy heart, and hath not given that blessing to thy neighbour; perhaps not to thy husband, thy wife, thy child, or thy parent. O what an obligation should this consideration lay upon thy heart greatly to fear the Lord! Remember also, as I have showed in the first part of this book, that this fear of the Lord is his treasure, a choice jewel, given only to favourites, and to those that are greatly beloved. Great gifts naturally tend to oblige, and will do so, I trust, with thee, when thou shalt ingeniously consider it. It is a sign of a very bad nature when the contrary shows itself; could God have done more for thee than to have put his fear in thy heart? This is better than to have given thee a place even in heaven without it. Yea, had he given thee all faith, all knowledge, and the tongue of men and angels, and a place in heaven to boot, they had all been short of this gift, of the fear of God in thy heart. Therefore love it, nourish it, exercise it, use all means to cause it to increase and grow in thy heart, that it may appear it is set by at thy hand, poor sinner.

Second. Another motive to stir thee up to grow in this grace of the fear of God may be the privileges that it lays thee under. What or where wilt thou find in the Bible, so many privileges so affectionately entailed to any grace, as to this of the fear of God? God speaks of this grace, and of the privileges that belong unto it, as if, to speak with reverence, he knew not how to have done blessing of the man that hath it. It seems to me as if this grace of fear is the darling grace, the grace that God sets his heart upon at the highest rate. As it were, he embraces the hugs, and lays the man in his bosom, that hath, and grows strong in this grace of the fear of God. See again the many privileges in which the man is interested that hath this grace in his heart: and see also that there are but few of them, wherever mentioned, but have entailed to them the pronunciation of a blessing, or else that man is spoken of by way of admiration.

Third. Another motive may be this: The man that groweth in this grace of the fear of the Lord will escape those evils that others will fall into. Where this grace is, it keepeth the soul from final apostasy, "I will put my fear in their hearts, that they shall not depart from me" (Jer 32:40). But yet, if there be not an increase in this grace, much evil may attend, and be committed notwithstanding. There is a child that is healthy, and hath its limbs, and can go, but it is careless; now the evil of carelessness doth disadvantage it very much; carelessness is the cause of stumblings, of falls, of knocks, and that it falls into the dirt, yea, that sometimes it is burned, or almost drowned. And thus it is, even with God's people that fear him, because they add not to their fear a care of growing more in the fear of God, therefore they reap damage; whereas, were they more in his fear, it would keep them better, deliver them more, and preserve them from these snares of death.

Fourth. Another motive may be this: To grow in this grace of the fear of God, is the way to be kept always in a conscientious performance of Christian duties. An increase in this grace, I say, keeps every grace in exercise, and the keeping of our graces in their due exercise, produceth a conscientious performance of duties. Thou hast a watch perhaps in thy pocket, but the hand will not as yet be kept in any good order, but does always give the lie as to the hour of the day; well, but what is the way to remedy this, but to look well to the spring, and the wheels within? for if they indeed go right, so will the hand do also. This is thy case in spiritual things; thou art a gracious man, and the fear of God is in thee, but yet for all that, one cannot well tell, by thy life, what time of day it is. Thou givest no true and constant sign that thou art indeed a Christian; why, the reason is, thou dost not look well to this grace of the fear of God. Thou dost not grow and increase in that, but sufferest thy heart to grow careless, and hard, and so thy life remiss and worldly: Job's growing great in the fear of God made him eschew evil (Job 1, 2:3).

Fifth. Another motive is: This is the way to be wise indeed. A wise man feareth and departeth from evil. It doth not say a wise man hath the grace of fear, but a wise man feareth, that is, putteth this grace into exercise. There is no greater sign of wisdom than to grow in this blessed grace. Is it not a sign of wisdom to depart from sins, which are the snares of death and hell? Is it not a sign of wisdom for a man yet more and more to endeavour to interest himself in the love and protection of God? Is it not a high point of wisdom for a man to be always doing of that which lays him under the conduct of angels? Surely this is wisdom. And if it be a blessing to have this fear, is it not wisdom to increase in it? Doubtless it is the highest point of wisdom, as I have showed before, therefore grow therein.

Sixth. Another motive may be this: It is seemly for saints to fear, and increase in this fear of God. He is thy Creator; is it not seemly for creatures to fear and reverence their Creator? He is thy King; is it not seemly for subjects to fear and reverence their King? He is thy Father; is it not seemly for children to reverence and fear their Father? yea, and to do it more and more?

Seventh. Another motive may be: It is honourable to grow in this grace of fear; "When Ephraim spake trembling, he exalted himself in Israel" (Hosea 13:1). Truly, to fear, and to about in this fear, is a sign of a very princely spirit; and the reason is, when I greatly fear my God, I am above the fear of all others, nor can anything in this world, be it never so terrible and dreadful, move me at all to fear them. And hence it is that Christ counsels us to fear— "And I say unto you, my friends," saith he, "be not afraid of them that kill the body, and after that have no more that they can do." Aye, but this is a high pitch, how should we come by such princely spirits? well, I will forewarn you whom you shall fear, and by fearing of him, arrive to this pitch, "Fear him, which after he hath killed, hath power to cast into hell; yea, I say unto you, fear him" (Luke 12:4,5). Indeed this true fear of God sets a man above all the world. And therefore it saith again, "Neither fear ye their fear," - but "sanctify the Lord God" in your hearts, "and let him be your fear, and let him be your dread" (Isa 8:12,13).

Your great ranting, swaggering, roysters, that are ignorant of the nature of the fear of God, count it a poor, sneaking, pitiful, cowardly spirit in men to fear and tremble before the Lord; but whoso looks back to jails and gibbets, to the sword and burning stake, shall see, that there, in them, has been the most mighty and invincible spirit that has been in the world!

Yea, see if God doth not count that the growth of his people in this grace of fear is that which makes them honourable, when he positively excludeth those from a dwelling-place in his house, that do not honour them that fear him (Psa 15:4). And he saith moreover, "A woman that feareth the Lord, she shall be praised." If the world and godless men will not honour these, they shall be honoured some way else. Such, saith he, "that honour me I will honour," and they shall be honoured in heaven, in the churches, and among the angels.

Eighth. Another motive to grow in this fear of God may be: This fear, and the increase of it, qualifies a man to be put in trust with heavenly and spiritual things, yea, and with earthly things too.

1. For heavenly and spiritual things. "My covenant," saith God, "was with [Levi] of life and peace, and I gave them to him, for the fear wherewith he feared me, and was afraid before my name" (Mal 2:5).

Behold what a gift, what a mercy, what a blessing this Levi is intrusted with; to wit, with God's everlasting covenant, and with the life and peace that is wrapped up in this covenant. But why is it given to him? the answer is, "for the fear wherewith he feared me, and was afraid before my name." And the reason is good, for this fear of God teaches a man to put a due estimation upon every gift of God bestowed upon us; also it teaches us to make use of the same with reverence of his name, and respect to his glory in most godly-wise, all which becomes him that is intrusted with any spiritual gift. The gift here was given to Levi to minister to his brethren doctrinally thereof, for he, saith God, shall teach Jacob my statutes and Israel my law. See also Exodus 18:21 and Nehemiah 7:2, with many other places that might be named, and you will find that men fearing God and hating covetousness; that men that fear God above others, are intrusted by God, yea, and by his church too, with the trust and ministration of spiritual things before any other in the world.

2. For earthly things. This fear of God qualifies a man to be put in trust with them rather than with another. Therefore God made Joseph lord of all Egypt; Obadiah, steward of Ahab's house; Daniel, Mordecai, and the three children, were set over the province of Babylon; and this by the wonderful working hand of God, because he had to dispose of earthly things now, not only in a common way, but for the good of his people in special. True, when there is no special matter or thing to be done by God in a nation for his people, then who will (that is, whether they have grace or no) may have the disposal of those things; but if God has anything in special to bestow upon his people of this world's goods, then he will intrust it in the hands of men fearing God. Joseph must now be made lord of Egypt, because Israel must be kept from starving; Obadiah must now be made steward of Ahab's house, because the Lord's prophets must be hid from and fed in despite of the rage and bloody mind of Jezebel; Daniel, with his companions, and Mordecai also, they were all exalted to earthly and temporal dignity, that they might in that state, they being men that abounded in the fear of God, be serviceable to their brethren in their straits and difficulties (Gen 42:18, 41:39; 1 Kings 18:3; Esth 6:10; Dan 2:48, 3:30, 5:29, 6:1-3).

Ninth. Another motive to grow in this grace of fear is, Where the fear of God in the heart of any is not growing, there no grace thrives, nor duty done as it should.

There no grace thrives, neither faith, hope, love, nor any grace. This is evident from that general exhortation, "Perfecting holiness in the fear of God" (2 Cor 7:1). Perfecting holiness, what is that? but as James says of patience, let every grace have its perfect work, that ye may be perfect and entire, lacking nothing (James 1:4).

But this cannot be done but in the fear of God, yea, in the exercise of that grace, and so consequently in the growth of it, for there is no grace but grows by being exercised. If then you would be perfect in holiness, if you would have every grace that God has put into your souls, grow and flourish into perfection; lay them, as I may say, a-soak in this grace of fear, and do all in the exercise of it; for a little done in the fear of the Lord is better than the revenues of the wicked. And again, the Lord will not suffer the soul of the righteous, the soul that liveth in the fear of the Lord, to famish, but he casteth away the abundance of the wicked. Bring abundance to God, and if it be not seasoned with godly fear, it shall not be acceptable to him, but loathsome and abominable in his sight; for it doth not flow from the spirit of the fear of the Lord.

Therefore, where there is not a growth in this fear, there is no duty done so acceptably. This flows from that which goes before, for if grace rather decays than grows, where this grace of fear is not in the growth and increase thereof, then duties in their glory and acceptableness decay likewise.

Tenth. Another motive to stir thee up to grow in the increase of this grace of fear is, It is a grace, do but abound therein, that will give thee great boldness both with God and men. Job was a man a none-such in his day for one that feared God; and who so bold with God as Job? who so bold with God, and who so bold with men as he? How bold was he with God, when he wishes for nothing more than that he might come even to his seat, and concludes that if he could come at him, he would approach even as a prince unto him, and as such would order his cause before him (Job 23:3-7, 31:35-37). Also before his friends, how bold was he? For ever as they laid to his charge that he was an hypocrite, he repels them with the testimony of a good conscience, which good conscience he got, and kept, and maintained by increasing in the fear of God; yea, his conscience was kept so good by this grace of fear, for it was by that that he eschewed evil, that it was common with him to appeal to God when accused, and also to put himself for his clearing under most bitter curses and imprecations (Job 13:3-9, 18, 19:23,24, 31).

This fear of God is it that keeps the conscience clean and tender, and so free from much of that defilement that even a good man may be afflicted with, for want of his growth in this fear of God. Yea, let me add, if a man can with a good conscience say that he desires to fear the name of God, it will add boldness to his soul in his approaches into the presence of God. "O Lord," said Nehemiah, "I beseech thee, let now thine ear be attentive to the prayer of thy servant, and servants, who desire to fear thy name" (Neh 1:11). He pleaded his desire of fearing the name of God, as an argument with God to grant him his request; and the reason was, because God had promised before "to bless them that fear him, both small and great" (Psa 115:13).

Eleventh. Another motive to stir you up to fear the Lord, and to grow in this fear is, By it thou mayest have thy labours blessed, to the saving of the souls of others. It is said of Levi, of whom mention was made before, that he feared God and was afraid before his name—that he saved others from their sins. "The law of truth was in his mouth, and he walked with me in peace and equity, and did turn away many from iniquity" (Mal 2:6). The fear of God that dwelt in his heart, showed its growth in the sanctifying of the Lord by his life and words, and the Lord also blessed this his growth herein, by blessing his labours to the saving of his neighbours.

Wouldest thou save thy husband, thy wife, thy children, &c., then be greatly in the fear of God.

This Peter teaches, "Wives," saith he, "be in subjection to your own husbands, that, if any obey not the word, they also may without the word be won by the conversation of the wives, while they behold your chaste conversation, coupled with fear" (1 Peter 3:1,2). So then, if wives and children, yea, if husbands, wives, children, servants, &c., did but better observe this general rule of Peter, to wit, of letting their whole conversation be coupled with fear, they might be made instruments in God's hand of much more good than they are. But the misery is, the fear of God is wanting in actions, and that is the cause that so little good is done by those that profess. It is not a conversation that is coupled with a profession—for a great profession may be attended with a life that is not good, but scandalous; but it is a conversation coupled with fear of God—that is, with the impressions of the fear of God upon it—that is convincing and that ministereth the awakenings of God to the conscience, in order to saving the unbeliever. O they are a sweet couple, to wit, a Christian conversation coupled with fear.

The want of this fear of God is that that has been a stumbling-block to the blind oftentimes. Alas, the world will not be convinced by your talk, by your notions, and by the great profession that you make, if they see not, therewith mixed, the lively impressions of the fear of God; but will, as I said, rather stumble and fall, even at your conversation and at your profession itself. Wherefore, to prevent this mischief, that is, of stumbling of souls while you make your profession of God, by a conversation not becoming your profession, God bids you fear him; implying that a good conversation, coupled with fear, delivers the blind world from those falls that otherwise they cannot be delivered from. "Thou shalt not curse the deaf, nor put a stumbling-block before the blind, but shalt fear thy God: I am the Lord" (Lev

19:14). But shalt fear thy God, that is the remedy that will prevent their stumbling at you, at what else soever they stumble. Wherefore Paul says to Timothy, "Take heed unto thyself, and unto the doctrine; continue in them; for in doing this thou shalt both save thyself and them that hear thee" (1 Tim 4:16).

Twelfth. Another motive to fear, and to grow in this fear of God is, This is the way to engage God to deliver thee from many outward dangers, whoever falls therein (Psa 34:7). This is proved from that of the story of the Hebrew midwives. "The midwives," said Moses, "feared God," and did not drown the men-children as the king had commanded, but saved them alive. And what follows? "Therefore God dealt well with the midwives; and it came to pass because the midwives feared God, that he made them houses" (Exo 1). That is, he sheltered them and caused them to be hid from the rage and fury of the king, and that perhaps in some of the houses of the Egyptians themselves for why might not the midwives be there hid as well as was Moses even in the king's court? And how many times are they that fear God said to be delivered both by God and his holy angels? as also I have already showed.

Thirteenth. Another motive to fear and to grow in this fear of God is, This is the way to be delivered from errors and damnable opinions. There are some that perish in their righteousness, that is an error; there be some that perish in their wickedness, and that is an error also. Some again prolong their lives by their wickedness, and others are righteous over-much, and also some are over-wise, and all these are snares, and pits, and holes. But then, sayest thou, how shall I escape? Indeed that is the question, and the Holy Ghost resolves it thus, "He that feareth God shall come forth of them all" (Eccl 7:18).

Fourteenth. Another motive to fear, and to grow in this fear of God, is, Such as have leave, be they never so dark in their souls, to come boldly to Jesus Christ, and to trust in him for life. I told you before, that they that fear God have in the general a license to trust in him; but now I tell you, and that in particular, that they, and they especially, may do it, and that though in the dark; you that sit in darkness and have no light, if this grace of fear be alive in your hearts, you have this boldness—"Who is among you that feareth the Lord," mark, that feareth the Lord, "that obeyeth the voice of his servant, that walketh in darkness, and hath no light? let him trust in the name of the Lord, and stay upon his God" (Isa 50:10). It is no small advantage, you know, when men have to deal in difficult matters, to have a patent or license to deal; now to trust in the Lord is a difficult thing, yet the best and most gainful of all. But then, some will say, since it is so difficult, how may we do without danger? Why, the text gives a license, a patent to them to trust in his name, that have his fear in their hearts—"Let him trust in the name of the

Lord, and stay upon his God."

Fifteenth. Another motive to fear and grow in this grace of fear, is, God will own and acknowledge such to be his, whoever he rejecteth. Yea he will distinguish and separate them from all others, in the day of his terrible judgments. He will do with them as he did by those that sighed for the abominations that were done in the land—command the man that hath his ink-horn by his side "to set a mark upon their foreheads," that they might not fall in that judgment with others (Eze 9). So God said plainly of them that feared the Lord, and that thought upon his name, that they should be writ in his book—"A book of remembrance was written before him for them that feared the Lord, and that thought upon his name; and they shall be mine, saith the Lord of hosts, in that day when I make up my jewels, and I will spare them as a man spareth his own son that serveth him" (Mal 3:16,17). Mark, he both acknowledges them for his, and also promises to spare them, as a man would spare his own son; yea, and moreover, will wrap them up as his chief jewels with himself in the bundle of life. Thus much for the motives.

How to grow in this fear of God.

Having given you these motives to the duty of growing in this fear of God, before I leave this use, I will, in a few words, show you how you may grow in this fear of God.

First. Then, if thou wouldest grow in this fear of God, learn aright to distinguish of fear in general. I mean, learn to distinguish between that fear that is godly, and that which in itself is indeed ungodly fear of God; and know them well the one from the other, lest the one, the fear that in itself indeed is ungodly, get the place, even the upper hand of that which truly is godly fear. And remember the ungodly fear of God is by God himself counted an enemy to him, and hurtful to his people, and is therefore most plentifully forbidden in the Word (Gen 3:15, 26:24, 46:3; Exo 14:13, 20:20; Num 14:9, 21:34; Isa 41:10,14, 43:1, 44:2,8; 54:4; Jer 30:10; Dan 10:12,19; Joel 2:21; Hagg 2:5; Zech 8:13).

Second. If thou wouldest grow in this godly fear, learn rightly to distinguish it from that fear, in particular, that is godly but for a time; even from that fear that is wrought by the Spirit, as a spirit of bondage. I say, learn to distinguish this from that, and also perfectly to know the bounds that God hath set to that fear that is wrought by the Spirit, as a spirit of bondage; lest, instead of growing in the fear that is to abide with thy soul for ever, thou be over-run again with that first fear, which is to abide with thee but till the spirit of adoption come. And that thou mayest not only distinguish them one from the other, but also keep each in its due place and bounds, consider in general of what hath already been said upon this head, and in particular that the first fear is no more wrought by the Holy Spirit, but by the devil, to distress thee, and make thee to live, not like a son, but a slave. And for thy better help in this matter, know that God himself hath set bounds to this fear, and has concluded that after the spirit of adoption is come, that other fear is wrought in thy heart by him no more (Rom 8:15; 2 Tim 1:7).

Again, before I leave this, let me tell thee that if thou dost not well bestir thee in this matter, this bondage fear, to wit, that which is like it, though not wrought in thee by the Holy Ghost, will, by the management and subtlety of the devil, the author of it, haunt, disturb, and make thee live uncomfortably, and that while thou art an heir of God and his kingdom. This is that fear that the apostle speaks of, that makes men "all their lifetime subject to bondage" (Heb 2:14,15). For though Christ will deliver thee indeed at last, thou having embraced him by faith, yet thy life will be full of trouble; and death, though Jesus hath abolished it, will be always a living bugbear to thee in all thy ways and thoughts, to break thy peace, and to make thee to draw thy loins heavily after him.

Third. Wouldest thou grow in this godly fear? then, as thou shouldest learn to distinguish of fears, so thou shouldest make conscience of which to entertain and cherish. If God would have his fear—and it is called HIS fear by way of eminency—"that his fear may be before you, that ye sin not" (Exo 20:20; Jer 32:40)—I say, if God would have his fear be with thee, then thou shouldest make conscience of this, and not so lightly give way to slavish fear, as is common for Christians to do.

There is utterly a fault among Christians about this thing; that is, they make not that conscience of resisting of slavish fear as they ought; they rather cherish and entertain it, and so weaken themselves, and that fear that they ought to strengthen.

And this is the reason that we so often lie grabbling under the black and amazing thoughts that are engendered in our hearts by unbelief; for this fear nourisheth unbelief; that is, now it doth, to wit, if we give way to it after the spirit of adoption is come, and readily closeth with all the fiery darts of the wicked.

But Christians are ready to do with this fear as the horse does when the tines of the fork are set against his side; even lean to it until it entereth into his belly. We lean naturally to this fear, I mean, after God has done good to our souls; it is hard striving against it, because it has even our sense and feeling of its side. But I say, if thou wouldest be a growing Christian—growing, I say, in the fear that is godly, in the fear that is always so—then make conscience of striving against the other, and against all these things that would bring thee back to it. "Wherefore should I fear," said David, "in the day of evil, when the iniquity of my heels shall compass me about?" (Psa 49:5).

What! not fear in the day of evil? What! not when the iniquity of thy heels compasseth thee about? No, not then, saith he, that is, not with that fear that would bring him again into bondage to the law; for he had received the spirit of adoption before. Indeed, if ever a Christian has ground to give way to slavish fear, it is at these two times, to wit, in the day of evil, and when the iniquity of his heels compasseth him about; but you see, David would not then, no, not then, give way thereto, nor did he see reason why he should. "Wherefore should I," said he? Aye, wherefore indeed? since now thou art become a son of God through Christ, and hast received the Spirit of his Son into thy heart, crying, Father, Father.

Fourth. Wouldest thou grow in this grace of godly fear? then grow in the knowledge of the new covenant, for that is indeed the girdle of our reins, and the strength of our souls. Hear what Zacharias saith: God, says he, "hath raised up an horn of salvation for us in the house of his servant David, as he spake by the mouth of his holy prophets which have been since the world began." But what was it? what was it that he spake? Why, "That he would grant unto us, that we, being delivered out of the hand of our enemies, might serve him without fear," without this slavish bondage fear, "in holiness and righteousness before him all the days of our life." But upon what is this princely fearless service of God grounded? Why, upon the holy covenant of God, upon the oath that he swore unto Abraham (Luke 1:69-74). Now in this covenant is wrapped up all thy salvation; in it is contained all thy desire, and I am sure, that then it containeth the complete salvation of thy soul; and I say, since this covenant is confirmed by promise, by oath, and by the blood of the Son of God, and that on purpose that thou mightest serve thy God without slavish fear, then the knowledge and faith of this covenant is of absolute necessity to bring us into this liberty, and out of our slavish terrors, and so, consequently, to cause us to grow in that son-like, godly fear, which became even the Son of God himself, and becomes all his disciples to live in the growth and exercise of.

Fifth. Wouldest thou grow in this godly fear? then labour even always to keep thine evidences for heaven and of thy salvation alive upon thy heart; for he that loseth his evidences for heaven, will hardly keep slavish fear out of heart; but he that hath the wisdom and grace to keep them alive, and apparent to himself, he will grow in this godly fear. See how David words it, "From the end of the earth," saith he, "will I cry unto thee; when my heart is overwhelmed, lead me to the rock that is higher than I. For thou hast been a shelter for me, and a strong tower from the enemy: I will abide in thy tabernacle for ever. For thou, O God, hast heard my vows; thou hast given me the heritage of those that fear thy name" (Psa 61:2-5). Mark a little, David doth by these words, in the first place, suggest that sometimes, to his thinking, he was as far off of his God as the ends of the earth are asunder, and that at such times he was subject to be overwhelmed, afraid: [And] second, the way that he took at such times, to help himself, was to cry to God to lead him again to Jesus Christ—"lead me to the rock that is higher than I" ; for indeed without faith in him, and the renewing of that faith, there can be no evidence for heaven made to appear unto the soul. This therefore he prays for first.

Then he puts that faith into exercise, and that with respect to the time that was past, and also of the time that was to come. For the time past, says he, "Thou hast been a shelter to me, and a strong tower from the enemy" ; and for the time to come, he said, "I will abide in thy tabernacle," that is, in thy Christ by faith, and in thy way of worship by love, "forever." And observe it, he makes the believing remembrance of his first evidences for heaven the ground of this his cry and faith, "For thou," says he, "O God, hast given me the heritage of those that fear thy name." Thou hast made me meet to be a partaker of the mercy of thy chosen, and hast put me under the blessing of goodness wherewith thou hast blessed those that fear thee. Thus you see how David, in his distresses, musters up his prayers, faith, and evidences for eternal life, that he might deliver himself from being overwhelmed, that is, with slavish fear, and that he might also abound in that son-like fear of his fellow-brethren, that is not only comely, with respect to our profession, but profitable to our souls.

Sixth. Wouldest thou grow in this fear of God? then set before thine eyes the being and majesty of God; for that both begetteth, maintaineth, and increaseth this fear. And hence it is called the fear of God, that is, an holy and awful dread and reverence of his majesty. For the fear of God is to stand in awe of him, but how can that be done if we do not set him before us? And again, if we would fear him more, we must abide more in the sense and faith of his glorious majesty. Hence this fear and God's name is so often put together: as fear God, fear the Lord, fear thy God, do this in the fear of the Lord, and thou shalt fear thy God, I am the Lord. For these words, "I am the Lord thy God," and the like, are on purpose put in, not only to show us whom we should fear, but also to beget, maintain, and increase in us that fear that is due from us to that "glorious and fearful name, the Lord our God" (Deut 28:58).

Seventh. Wouldest thou grow in this grace of fear? then keep always close to thy conscience the authority of the Word; fear the commandment as the commandment of a God both mighty and glorious, and as the commandment of a father, both loving and pitiful; let this commandment, I say, be always with thine eye, with thine ear, and with thine heart; for then thou wilt be taught, not only to fear, but to abound in the fear of the Lord. Every grace is nourished by the Word, and without it there is no thrift in the soul (Prov 13:13, 4:20-22; Deut 6:1,2).

Eighth. Wouldest thou grow in this grace of fear? then be much in the faith of the promise, of the promise that maketh over to thy soul an interest in God by Christ, and of all good things. The promise naturally tendeth to increase in us the fear of the Lord, because this fear, it grows by goodness and mercy; they shall fear the Lord, and his goodness; now this goodness and mercy of God, it is wrapt up in, and made over to us by promise; for God gave it to Abraham by promise. Therefore the faith and hope of the promise causeth this fear to grow in the soul—"Having therefore these promises, dearly beloved, let us cleanse ourselves from all filthiness of the flesh and spirit, perfecting holiness in the fear of God" (2 Cor 7:1). "Perfecting holiness in the fear of God" ; therefore that fear by the promise must needs grow mighty, for by, with, and in it, you see holiness is perfected.

Ninth. Wouldest thou grow in this grace of fear? then remember the judgments of God that have, or shall certainly overtake, those professors, that have either been downright hypocrites, or else unwatchful Christians. For both these sorts partake of the judgments of God; the one, to wit, the true Christian, for his unwatchfulness, for his correction; the other, to wit, the hypocrite, for his hypocrisy, to his destruction. This is a way to make thee stand in awe, and to make thee tremble, and grow in the grace of fear before thy God.

Judgments! you may say, what judgments? Answ. Time will fail me here to tell thee of the judgments that sometimes overtake God's people, and that always certainly overtake the hypocrite for his transgressions. For those that attend God's people, I would have thee look back to the place in this book where they are particularly touched upon. And for those that attend the hypocrite, in general they are these. 1. Blindness of heart in this world. 2. The death of their hope at the day of their death. 3. And the damnation of their souls at the day of judgment (Matt 23:15-19; Job 8:13, 11:20, 18:14, 20:4-7, Matt 23:33, 24:51; Luke 20:47). The godly consideration of these things tend to make men grow in the fear of God.

Tenth. Wouldest thou grow in this grace of fear? then study the excellencies of the grace of fear, and what profit it yieldeth to them that have it, and labour to get thy heart into the love, both of the exercise of the grace itself, and also of the fruit it yieldeth; for a man hardly grows in the increase of any grace, until his heart is united to it, and until it is made lovely in his eyes (Psa 119:119,120). Now the excellencies of this grace of fear have also been discoursed of in this book before, where by reading thou shalt find the fruit it bears, and the promises that are annexed to it, which, because they are many, I refer thee also thither for thy instruction.

Eleventh. Wouldest thou grow in this grace of fear? then remember what a world of privileges do belong to them that fear the Lord, as also I have hinted; namely, that such shall not be hurt, shall want no good thing, shall be guarded by angels, and have a special license, though in never so dreadful a plight, to trust in the name of the Lord, and stay upon their God.

Twelfth. Wouldest thou grow in this grace of fear? then be much in prayer to God for abundance of the increase thereof. To fear God is that which is according to his will, and if we ask anything according to his will, he heareth us. Pray therefore that God will unite thy heart to fear his name; this is the way to grow in the grace of fear.

Lastly, Wouldest thou grow in this grace of fear? then devote thyself to it (Psa 119:38). Devote myself to it, you will say, how is that? I answer, why, give thyself to it, addict thyself to it. Solace thyself in the contemplation of God, and of a reverence of his name, and word, and worship. Then wilt thou fear, and grow in this grace of fear.

What things they are that have a tendency in them to hinder the growth of the fear of God in our hearts.

And that I may yet be helpful to thee, reader, I shall now give thee caution of those things that will, if way be given to them, hinder thy growth in this fear of God, the which, because they are very hurtful to the people of God, I would have thee be warned by them. And they are these which follow:

First. If thou wouldest grow in this grace of fear, take heed of A HARD HEART, for that will hinder thy growth in this grace. "Why hast thou hardened our heart from thy fear?" was a bitter complaint of the church heretofore; for it is not only the judgment that in itself is dreadful and sore to God's people, but that which greatly hindereth the growth of this grace in the soul (Isa 63:17). A hard heart is but barren ground for any grace to grow in, especially for the grace of fear: there is but little of this fear where the heart is indeed hard; neither will there ever be much therein.

Now if thou wouldest be kept from a hard heart, 1. Take heed of the beginnings of sin. Take heed, I say, of that, though it should be never so small; "A little leaven leaveneth the whole lump." There is more in a little sin to harden, than in a great deal of grace to soften. David's look upon Bathsheba was, one would think, but a small matter; yet that beginning of sin contracted such hardness of heart in him, that it carried him almost beyond all fear of God. It did carry him to commit lewdness with her, murder upon the body of Uriah, and to abundance of wicked dissimulation; which are things, I say, that have direct tendency to quench and destroy all fear of God in the soul.

2. If thou hast sinned, lie not down without repentance; for the want of repentance, after one has sinned, makes the heart yet harder and harder. Indeed a hard heart is impenitent, and impenitence also makes the heart harder and harder. So that if impenitence be added to hardness of heart, or to the beginning of sin which makes it so, it will quickly be with that soul, as is said of the house of Israel, it will have a whore's forehead, it will hardly be brought to shame (Jer 3:3).

3. If thou wouldest be rid of a hard heart, that great enemy to the growth of the grace of fear, be much with Christ upon the cross in thy meditations; for that is an excellent remedy against hardness of heart: a right sight of him, as he hanged there for thy sins, will dissolve thy heart into tears, and make it soft and tender. "They shall look upon me whom they have pierced, - and mourn" (Zech 12:10). Now a soft, a tender, and a broken heart, is a fit place for the grace of fear to thrive in. But,

Second. If thou wouldest have the grace of fear to grow in thy soul, take heed also of A PRAYERLESS HEART, for that is not a place for this grace of fear to grow in. Hence he that restraineth prayer is said to cast off fear. "Thou castest off fear," said one of his friends to Job. But how must he do that? Why the next words show, "Thou restrainest prayer before God" (Job 15:4). Seest thou a professor that prayeth not? that man thrusteth the fear of God away from him. Seest thou a man that prays but little, that man feareth God but little; for it is the praying soul, the man that is mighty in praying, that has a heart for the fear of God to grow in. Take heed, therefore, of a prayerless heart, if you would grow in this grace of the fear of God. Prayer is as the pitcher that fetcheth water from the brook, therewith to water the herbs; break the pitcher, and it will fetch no water, and for want of water the garden withers.

Third. Wouldest thou grow in this grace of fear? then take heed of A LIGHT AND WANTON HEART, for neither is such a heart good ground for the fear of God to grow in. Wherefore it is said of Israel, "She feared not, but went and played the harlot also." She was given to wantonness, and to be light and vain, and so her fear of God decayed (Jer 3:8). Had Joseph been as wanton as his mistress, he had been as void of the fear of God as she; but he was of a sober, tender, godly, considerate spirit, therefore he grew in the fear of God.

Fourth. Wouldest thou grow in this grace of fear? then take heed of A COVETOUS HEART, for neither is that which is such an one good ground for this grace of fear to grow in. Therefore this covetousness and the fear of God are as enemies, set the one in opposition to the other: one that feareth God and hateth covetousness (Exo 18:21). And the reason why covetousness is such an obstruction to the growth of this grace of fear, is because covetousness casteth those things out of the heart which alone can nourish this fear. It casteth out the Word and love of God, without which no grace can grow in the soul; how then should the fear of God grow in a covetous heart? (Eze 33:30-32; 1 John 2:15).

Fifth. Wouldest thou grow in this grace of fear? then take heed of AN UNBELIEVING HEART, for an unbelieving heart is not good ground for this grace of fear to grow in. An unbelieving heart is called "an evil heart," because from it flows all the wickedness that is committed in the world (Heb 3:12). Now it is faith, or a believing heart, that nourisheth this fear of God, and not the other; and the reason is, for that faith brings God, heaven, and hell, to the soul, and maketh it duly consider of them all (Heb 11:7). This is therefore the means of fear, and that which will make it grow in the soul; but unbelief is a bane thereto.

Sixth. Wouldest thou grow in this grace of fear? then take heed of A FORGETFUL HEART. Such a heart is not a heart where the grace of fear will flourish, "when I remember, I am afraid," &c. Therefore take heed of forgetfulness; do not forget but remember God, and his kindness, patience, and mercy, to those that yet neither have grace, nor special favour from him, and that will beget and nourish his fear in thy heart, but forgetfulness of this, or of any other of his judgments, is a great wound and weakening to this fear (Job 21:6). When a man well remembers that God's judgments are so great a deep and mystery, as indeed they are, that remembrance puts a man upon such considerations of God and of his judgments as to make him fear— "Therefore," said Job, "I am afraid of him." See the place, Job 23:15.

"Therefore am I troubled at his presence; when I consider, I am afraid of him"—when I remember and consider of the wonderful depths of his judgments towards man.

Seventh. Wouldest thou grow in this grace of fear? then take heed of A MURMURING AND REPINING HEART, for that is not a heart for this grace of fear to grow in. As for instance, when men murmur and repine at God's hand, at his dispensations, and at the judgments that overtake them, in their persons, estates, families, or relations, that their murmuring tendeth to destroy fear; for a murmuring spirit is such an one as seems to correct God, and to find fault with his dispensations, and where there is that, the heart is far from fear. A murmuring spirit either comes from that wisdom that pretends to understand that there is a failure in the nature and execution of things, or from an envy and spite at the execution of them. Now if murmurings arise from this pretended wisdom of the flesh, then instead of fearing of God, his actions are judged to be either rigid or ridiculous, which yet are done in judgment, truth, and righteousness. So that a murmuring heart cannot be a good one for the fear of God to grow in. Alas! the heart where that grows must be a soft one; as you have it in Job 23:15, 16; and a heart that will stoop and be silent at the most abstruse of all his judgments—"I was dumb, because THOU didst it." The heart in which this fear of God doth flourish is such, that it bows and is mute, if it can but espy the hand, wisdom, justice, or holiness of God in this or the other of his dispensations, and so stirs up the soul to fear before him. But if this murmuring ariseth from envy and spite, that looketh so like to the spirit of the devil, that nothing need be said to give conviction of the horrible wickedness of it.

Eighth. Wouldest thou grow in this grace of fear? then take heed of A HIGH AND CAPTIOUS SPIRIT, for that is not good ground for the fear of God to grow in. A meek and quiet spirit is the best, and there the fear of God will flourish most; therefore Peter puts meekness and fear together, as being most suited in their nature and natural tendency one to another (1 Peter 3:15). Meekness of spirit is like that heart that hath depth of earth in it in which things may take root and grow; but a high and captious spirit is like to the stony ground, where there is not depth of earth, and consequently, where this grace of fear cannot grow; therefore take heed of this kind of spirit, if thou wouldest that the fear of God should grow in thy soul.

Ninth. Wouldest thou grow in this grace of fear? then take heed of AN ENVIOUS HEART, for that is not a good heart for the fear of God to grow in. "Let not thine heart envy sinners; but be thou in the fear of the Lord all the day long" (Prov 23:17). To envy any is a sign of a bad spirit, and that man takes upon him, as I have already hinted, to be a controller and a judge, yea, and a malicious executioner too, and that of that fury that ariseth from his own lusts and revengeful spirit, upon (perhaps) the man that is more righteous than himself. But suppose he is a sinner that is the object of thine envy, why, the text sets that envy in direct opposition to the fear of God; "Envy not sinners, but be thou in the fear of God." These two, therefore, to wit, envy to sinners and fearing of God, are opposites. Thou canst not fear God, and envy sinners too. And the reason is, because he that envieth a sinner, hath forgotten himself, that he is as bad; and how can he then fear God? He that envies sinners rejects his duty of blessing of them that curse, and praying for them that despitefully use us; and how can he that hath rejected this, fear God? He that envieth sinners, therefore, cannot be of a good spirit, nor can the fear of God grow in his heart.

Tenth. Lastly, Wouldest thou grow in this grace of fear? then take heed of HARDENING THY HEART at any time against convictions to particular duties, as to prayer, alms, self-denial, or the like. Take heed also of hardening thy heart, when thou art under any judgment of God, as sickness, losses, crosses, or the like. I bid you before to beware of a hard heart, but now I bid you beware of hardening your soft ones. For to harden the heart is to make it worse than it is; harder, more desperate, and bold against God, than at the present it is. Now, I say, if thou wouldest grow in this grace of fear, take heed of hardening thy heart, and especially of hardening of it against convictions to good; for those convictions are sent of God like seasonable showers of rain, to keep the tillage of thy heart in good order, that the grace of fear may grow therein; but this stifling of convictions makes the heart as hard as a piece of the nether millstone. Therefore happy is he that receiveth conviction, for so he doth keep in the fear of God, and that fear thereby nourished in his soul; but cursed is he that doth otherwise—"Happy is the man that feareth alway; but he that hardeneth his heart shall fall into mischief" (Prov 28:14).

USE THIRD, of encouragement.

USE THIRD. I come now to A USE OF ENCOURAGEMENT to those that are blessed with this grace of fear. The last text that was mentioned saith, "Happy is the man that feareth alway," and so doth many more. Happy already, because blessed with this grace; and happy for time to come, because this grace shall abide, and continue till the soul that hath it is brought unto the mansion-house of glory. "I will put my fear in their hearts, that they shall not depart from me." Therefore, as here it saith, Happy is he, so it saith also, It shall go well with him, that is, in time to come. "It shall be well with them that fear God" (Eccl 8:12).

First. Had God given thee all the world, yet cursed hadst thou been, if he had not given thee the fear of the Lord; for the fashion of this world is a fading thing, but he that feareth the Lord shall abide for ever and ever. This therefore is the first thing that I would propound for thy encouragement, thou man that fears the Lord. This grace will dwell in thy heart, for it is a new covenant grace, and will abide with thee for ever. It is sent to thee from God, not only to join thy heart unto him, but to keep thee from final apostasy—"I will put my fear in their hearts, that they shall not depart from me" (Jer 32:40). That thou mayest never forsake God, is his design, and therefore, to keep thee from that wicked thing, he hath put his fear in thy heart. Many are the temptations, difficulties, snares, traps, trials, and troubles that the people of God pass through in the world, but how shall they be kept, how shall they be delivered, and escape? Why, the answer is, The fear of God will keep them—"He that feareth God shall come forth of them all."

Is it not therefore a wonderful mercy to be blessed with this grace of fear, that thou by it mayest be kept from final, which is damnable apostasy? Bless God, therefore, thou blessed man, that hast this grace of fear in thy soul. There are five things in this grace of fear that have a direct tendency in them to keep thee from final apostasy.

1. It is seated in the heart, and the heart is, as I may call it, the main fort in the mystical world, man. It is not placed in the head, as knowledge is; nor in the mouth, as utterance is, but in the heart, the seat of all, "I will put my fear in their hearts." If a king will keep a town secure to himself, let him be sure to man sufficiently the main fort thereof. If he have twenty thousand men well armed, yet if they lie scattered here and there, the town may be taken for all that, but if the main fort be well manned, then the town is more secure. What if a man had all the parts, yea, all the arts of men and angels? That will not keep the heart to God. But when the heart, this principal fort, is possessed with the fear of God, then he is safe, but not else.

2. As the heart in general, so the will in special. That chief and great faculty of the soul is the principle that is acted by this fear. The will, which way that goes, all goes; if it be to heaven or hell. Now the will, I say, is that main faculty that is governed by this fear that doth possess the soul, therefore all is like to go well with it. This Samuel insinuateth, where he saith, "If ye will fear the Lord." Fearing of God is a voluntary act of the will, and that being so, the soul is kept from rebellion against the commandment, because by the will where this fear of God is placed, and which it governeth, is led all the rest of the powers of the soul (1 Sam 12:14). In this will, then, is this fear of God placed, that this grace may the better be able to govern the soul, and so by consequence the whole man; for as I said before, look what way the will

goes, look what the will does, thither goes, and that does, the whole man (Psa 110:3). Man, when his will is alienate from God, is reckoned rebellious throughout, and that not without ground, for the will is the principal faculty of the soul as to obedience, and therefore things done without the will are as if they were not done at all. The spirit is willing; if ye be willing; "she hath done what she could," and the like; by these and such- like sayings the goodness of the heart and action is judged, as to the subjective part thereof. Now this fear that we have been speaking of, is placed in the soul, and so consequently in the will, that the man may thereby the better be kept from final and damnable apostasy.

3. This fear, as I may say, even above every other grace, is God's well-wisher; and hence it is called, as I also have showed you, his fear. As he also says in the text mentioned above, "I will put my fear in their hearts." These words, his and my, they are intimate and familiar expressions, bespeaking not only great favour to man, but a very great trust put in him. As who should say, this fear is my special friend, it will subject and bow the soul, and the several faculties thereof, to my pleasure; it is my great favourite, and subdueth sinners to my pleasure. You shall rarely find faith or repentance, or parts, go under such familiar characters as this blessed fear of the Lord doth. Of all the counsellors and mighties that David had, Hushai only was called the king's friend (2 Sam 15:37, 16:16). So of all the graces of the Spirit this of the fear of God goes mostly, if not always, by the title of MY fear, God's fear, HIS fear, &c. I told you before, if the king will keep a town, the main fort therein must be sufficiently manned: and now I will add, that if he have not to govern those men some trusty and special friend, such as Hushai was to David, he may find it lost when it should stand him in greatest stead. If a soul should be possessed with all things possible, yet if this fear of God be wanting, all other things will give place in time of rebellion, and the soul shall be found in, and under the conduct of hell, when it should stand up for God and his truth in the world. This fear of God, it is God's special friend, and therefore it has given unto it the chief seat of the heart, the will, that the whole man may now be, and also be kept hereafter, in the subjection and obedience of the gospel. For,

4. This grace of fear is the softest and most tender of God's honour of any other grace. It is that tender, sensible, and trembling grace, that keepeth the soul upon its continual watch. To keep a good watch is, you know, a wonderful safety to a place that is in continual danger because of the enemy. Why, this is the grace that setteth the watch, and that keepeth the watchmen awake (Can 3:7,8). A man cannot watch as he should, if he be destitute of fear: let him be confident, and he sleeps; he unadvisedly lets into the garrison those that should not come there. Israel's fault when they came to Canaan

was, that they made a covenant with the inhabitants of the land, to wit, the Gibeonites, without asking counsel of God. But would they have done so, think you, if at the same time the fear of God had had its full play in the soul, in the army? no, they at that time forgot to fear. The grace of fear had not at that time its full stroke and sway among them.

5. This grace of fear is that which, as I may so say, first affects the hearts of saints with judgments, after we have sinned, and so is as a beginning grace to bring again that to rights that by sin is put out of frame. O it is a precious grace of God! I know what I say in this matter, and also where I had been long ago, through the power of my lusts, and the wiles of the devil, had it not been for the fear of God.

Second. But secondly, another encouragement for those that are blessed with this blessed grace of fear is this,—this fear fails not to do this work for the soul, if there in truth, be it never so small in measure. A little of this leaven "leaveneth the whole lump." True, a little will not do, or help the soul to do those worthy exploits in the heart or life as well as a bigger measure thereof; nor, indeed, can a little of any grace do that which a bigger measure will; but a little will preserve the soul from final apostasy, and deliver it into the arms of the Son of God at the final judgment. Wherefore, when he saith, "I will put my fear in their hearts," he says not, I will put so much of it there, such a quantity, or such a degree; but, "I will put my fear there." I speak not this in the least to tempt the godly man to be content with the least degree of the fear of God in his heart. True, men should be glad that God hath put even the least degree of this grace into their souls, but they should not be content therewith; they should earnestly covet more, pray for more, and use all lawful, that is, all the means of God's appointing, that they may get more.

There are, as I have said already, several degrees of this grace of fear, and our wisdom is to grow in it, as in all the other graces of the Spirit. The reasons why, I have showed you, and also the way to grow therein; but the least measure thereof will do as I said, that is, keep the soul from final apostasy. There are, as I have showed you, those that greatly fear the Lord, that fear exceedingly, and that fear him above many of their brethren; but the small in this grace are saved as well as those that are great therein: "He will bless" or save "them that fear him, both small and great." This fear of the Lord is the pulse of the soul; and as some pulses beat stronger, some weaker, so is this grace of fear in the soul. They that beat best are a sign of best life, but they that beat worst show that life is [barely] present. As long as the pulse beats, we count not that the man is dead, though weak; and this fear, where it is, preserves to everlasting life. Pulses there are also that are intermitting; to wit, such as have their times for a little, a little time to stop, and beat again; true, these are dangerous pulses, but yet too a sign of life. This fear of God also is sometimes like this intermitting pulse; there are times when it forbears to work, and then it works again. David had an intermitting pulse, Peter had an intermitting pulse, as also many other of the saints of God. I call that an intermitting pulse, with reference to the fear we speak of, when there is some obstruction by the workings of corruptions in the soul; I say, some obstruction from, and hindrance of, the continual motion of this fear of God; yet none of these, though they are various, and some of them signs of weakness, are signs of death, but life. "I will put my fear in their hearts, that they shall not depart from me."

Quest. But you may say, How shall I know that I fear God?

Answ. If I should say that desires, true sincere desires to fear him, is fear itself. I should not say amiss (Neh 1:11). For although a desire to be, or do so and so, makes not a man to be in temporal or natural things what he desires to be—for a sick, or poor, or imprisoned man may desire to be well, to be rich, or to be at liberty, and yet be as they are, sick, poor, or in prison—yet in spirituals, a man's desire to be good, to believe, to love, to hope, and fear God, doth flow from the nature of grace itself.

I said before, that in temporals a man could not properly be said to be what he was not; yet a man, even in naturals or temporals, shows his love to that thing that he desires, whether it be health, riches, or liberty; and in spirituals, desires of, from love to this or that grace of God, sincere desires of it flow from the root of the grace itself—"Thy servants who desire to fear thy name." Nehemiah bore himself before God upon this, "that he desired to fear his name." And hence again it is said concerning desires, true desires, "The desire of man is his kindness" (Prov 19:22). For a man shows his heart, his love, his affections, and his delights, in his desires; and since the grace of the fear of God is a grace so pleasant in the sight of God, and of so sanctifying a nature in the soul where it is, a true sincere desire to be blessed with that grace must needs flow from some being of this grace in the soul already.

True desires are lower than higher acts of grace, but God will not overlook desires—"But now they desire a better country, that is, an heavenly; wherefore God is not ashamed to be called their God; for he hath prepared for them a city." Mark, they desire a country, and they shall have a city. At this low place, to wit, sincere desires, God will meet the soul and will tell him that he hath accepted of his desires, that his desires are his kindness, and flow from grace itself: "He will fulfil the desire of them that fear him." Therefore desires are not rejected of God; but they would, if they did not flow from a principle of grace already in the soul; therefore desires, sincere desires to fear God, flow from grace already in the soul. Therefore, since thou fearest God, and it is evident by thy desires that thou dost so do, thou art happy now in this thy fear, and shalt be happy for ever hereafter in the enjoyment of that which God in another world hath laid up for them that fear him.

Third. Another encouragement for those that have this grace of fear is this; this grace can make that man, that in many other things is not capable of serving of God, serve him better than those that have all without it. Poor Christian man, thou hast scarce been able to do anything for God all thy days, but only to fear the Lord. Thou art no preacher, and so canst not do him service that way; thou art no rich man, and so canst not do him service with outward substance; thou art no wise man, and so canst not do anything that way; but here is thy mercy, thou fearest God. Though thou canst not preach, thou canst fear God. Though thou hast no bread to feed the belly, nor fleece to clothe the back of the poor, thou canst fear God. O how "blessed is the man that feareth the Lord" ; because this duty of fearing of God is an act of the mind, and may be done by the man that is destitute of all things but that holy and blessed mind.

Blessed therefore is that man, for God hath not laid the comfort of his people in the doing of external duties, nor the salvation of their souls, but in believing, loving, and fearing God. Neither hath he laid these things in actions done in their health nor in the due management of their most excellent parts, but in the receiving of Christ, and fear of God. The which, good Christian, thou mayest do, and do acceptably, even though thou shouldest lie bed-rid all thy days; thou mayest also be sick and believe; be sick and love, be sick and fear God, and so be a blessed man. And here the poor Christian hath something to answer them that reproach him for his ignoble pedigree, and shortness of the glory of the wisdom of the world. True, may that man say, I was taken out of the dunghill, I was born in a base and low estate, but I fear God. I have no worldly greatness, nor excellency of natural parts, but I fear God.

When Obadiah met with Elijah, he gave him no worldly and fantastical compliment, nor did he glory in his promotion by Ahab the king of Israel, but gravely, and after a gracious manner, said, "I thy servant fear the Lord from my youth." Also when the mariners inquired of Jonah, saying, "What is thine occupation, and whence comest thou? what is thy country, and of what people art thou?" This was the answer he gave them, "I am a Hebrew, and I fear the Lord, the God of heaven, which hath made the sea and the dry land" (Jonah 1:8,9). Indeed this answer is the highest, and most noble in the world, nor are there any, save a few, that in truth can thus express themselves, though other answers they had enough; most can say, I have wisdom, or might, or riches, or friends, or health, or the like; these are common, and are greatly boasted in by the most; but he is the man that feareth God, and he that can say, when they say to him, What art thou? "I thy servant fear the Lord," he is the man of many, he is to be honoured of men: though this, to wit, that he feareth the Lord, is all that he hath in the world. He hath the thing, the honour, the life, and glory that is lasting; his blessedness will abide when all men's but his is buried in the dust, in shame and contempt.

A word to hypocrites.

Hypocrites, my last word is to you; the hypocrite is one that would appear to be that in men's eyes that is nothing of in God's—thou hypocrite, that wouldest be esteemed to be one that loves and that fears God, but does not; I have this to say to thee, thy condition is damnable, because thou art a hypocrite, and seekest to

deceive both God and man with guises, vizards, masks, shows, pretences, and thy formal, carnal, feigned subjection to the outside of statutes, laws, and commandments; but within thou art full of rottenness and all excess.

Hypocrite, thou mayest by thy cunning shifts be veiled and hid from men, but thou art naked before the eyes of God, and he knoweth that his fear is not in thy heart (Luke 16:15).

Hypocrite, be admonished that there is not obedience accepted of God, where the heart is destitute of this grace of fear. Keeping of the commandments is but one part of the duty of man, and Paul did that, even while he was a hypocrite (Phil 3). To "fear God and keep his commandments, this is the whole duty of man" (Eccl 12:13). This—fear God—the hypocrite, as a hypocrite, cannot do, and therefore, as such, cannot escape the damnation of hell.

Hypocrite, thou must fear God first, even before thou dost offer to meddle with the commandments, that is, as to the keeping of them. Indeed, thou shouldest read therein, that thou mayest learn to fear the Lord, but yet, "fear God" goes before the command to keep his commandments. And if thou dost not fear God first, thou transgressest, instead of keeping of the commandments.

Hypocrite, this word, FEAR GOD, is that which the hypocrite quite forgets, although it is that which sanctifies the whole duty of man. For this is that, and nothing without it, that can make a man sincere in his obedience; the hypocrite looks for applause abroad, and forgets that he is condemned at home, and both these he does because he wanteth the fear of God.

Hypocrite, be admonished that none of the privileges that are spoken of in the former part of the book belongs to thee, because thou art a hypocrite; and if thou hope, thy hope shall be cut off, and if thou lean upon thy house, both thou and it shall fall into hell-fire. Triumph then, thy triumph is but for awhile. Joy then, but the joy of the hypocrite is but for a moment (Job 8:13,15, 20:4-6).

Perhaps thou wilt not let go now, what, as a hypocrite, thou hast got; but "what is the hope of the hypocrite, when God taketh away his soul?" (Job 27:8). Hypocrite, thou shouldest have chosen the fear of God, as thou hast chosen a profession without it, but thou hast cast off fear, because thou art a hypocrite; and because thou art such, thou shalt have the same measure that thou metest; God will cast thee off, because thou art a hypocrite. God hath prepared a fear for thee because thou didst not choose the fear of God, and that fear shall come upon thee like desolation, and like an armed man, and shall swallow thee up, thou and all that thou art (Prov 1:27).

Hypocrite, read this text and tremble—"The sinners in Zion are afraid, fearfulness hath surprised the hypocrites. Who among us shall dwell with the devouring fire? who among us shall dwell with everlasting burnings?" (Isa 33:13,14).

Hypocrite, thou art not under the fatherly protection of God, because thou art a hypocrite, and wantest his fear in thine heart. The eyes of the Lord are upon them that fear him, to deliver them. But the fearless man or hypocrite is left to the snares and wiles of the devil, to be caught therein and overcome, because he is destitute of the fear of God.

Hypocrite, thou art like to have no other reward of God for thy labour than that which the goats shall have; the hypocrite, because he is a hypocrite, shall not stand in God's sight. The gain of thy religion thou spendest as thou gettest it. Thou wilt not have one farthing overplus at death and judgment.

Hypocrite, God hath not intrusted thee with the least dram of his saving grace, nor will he, because thou art a hypocrite: and as for what thou hast, thou hast stolen it, even every man of you from his neighbour; still pilfering out of their profession, even as Judas did out of the bag. Thou comest like a thief into thy profession, and like a thief thou shalt go out of the same. Jesus Christ hath not counted thee faithful to commit to thee any of his jewels to keep, because thou fearest him not. He hath given his "banner to them that fear him, that it may be displayed because of the truth" (Psa 60:4).

Hypocrite, thou art not true to God nor man, nor thine own soul, because thou art a hypocrite! How should the Lord put any trust in thee? Why should the saints look for any good from thee? Should God give thee his Word, thou wilt sell it. Should men commit their souls to thee, thou wilt destroy them, by making merchandise of them, for thy own hypocritical designs. Yea, if the sun waxes hot, thou wilt throw all away, and not endure the heat, because thou art a hypocrite!

Made in the USA
Middletown, DE
26 December 2022